DIVERSITY
AT
COLLEGE

DIVERSITY

AT

COLLEGE

Real stories of students conquering bias and making higher education more inclusive.

James Stellar, Chrisel Martinez, Brandy Eggan, Beny Poy,
Chloe' Skye Weiser, Rachel Eager, Marc Cohen, Agata Buras

IDEAPRESS
PUBLISHING

IS THIS BOOK FOR YOU?

If you've picked up this book, you know that we as a society are reckoning with racism, xenophobia, and many other forms of societal division. The fault belongs to no one individually, but each individual has the power to challenge the status quo and advocate for change.

This book contains five personal stories from [former] college students who challenged the status quo and advocated for a more inclusive higher education experience. College campuses can often be the first environment where students leave the communities they grew up in and encounter diversity of race, gender, and language. It is important to understand how diversity plays a big role in everyday life and how our minds contribute to it. We have an unconscious mind that governs our decisions, direct experience is one of the best ways to promote the benefits diversity brings to our society. Bias exists, whether we recognize it or not. With time, effort, and the willingness to insert yourself in different experiences we can retrain the mind to address unconscious biases. People can change - and in turn, create a stronger and more equitable society where all members have a seat at the table.

You're part of this important work - Be kind to yourself in this process but be committed.

See you on the first page.

IDEAPRESS
PUBLISHING

Published in the United States by Ideapress Publishing.

Ideapress Publishing | www.ideapresspublishing.com

Cover Design by Amanda Hudson, Faceout Studios

Interior Design by Jessica Angerstein

The authors wish to thank Elizabeth Gray for valuable design and editorial assistance in the preparation of this work.

Cataloging-in-Publication Data is on file with the Library of Congress.

ISBN: 978-1-64687-035-6 (Paperback)

SPECIAL SALES

Ideapress books are available at a special discount for bulk purchases for sales promotions or corporate training programs. Special editions, including personalized covers and custom forewords, are also available. For more details, email info@ideapresspublishing.com or contact the author directly.

CONTENTS

PREFACE i

CHAPTER 1 1
INTRODUCTION AND OVERVIEW

CHAPTER 2 23
BENY'S STORY | Implicit Bias
*Philosophy: A field of white men with white
beards pondering white people problems*

CHAPTER 3 37
RACHEL'S STORY | Self-handicapping
Women in Science

CHAPTER 4: 49
CHRISEL'S STORY | Low Socioeconomic Status
and Peer Support
Defying Gravity

CHAPTER 5 65
MARC'S STORY | In-group/Out-group
Find Your Niche

CHAPTER 6 81
AGATA'S STORY | Stereotype Threat
The Fear of Starting Over

CHAPTER 7 95
CONCLUSIONS
Experiential Education in Leveraging Diversity

APPENDIX 135
Brief bios and notes to the reader from each co-author

PREFACE

Universities and colleges have always played an important role in shaping the future. They push us forward through discovery, technological advances, creative expression, innovation across disciplines, and perhaps most importantly, through the education of their students. Along with the overall growth over the last few decades in the number of students who continue on to higher education, there has also been a change in the profile of the student body. These students reflect the demographic changes in America, as we shift into greater diversity of ethnic and racial backgrounds, increasing income and wealth inequality, a markedly enhanced use of social media and online technology, greater concern for climate change, a new gig-economy perspective on work and career, and more. It is important that institutions of higher education evolve alongside the transformations of their student bodies. In this book, we will address how higher education can serve its increasingly diverse population of undergraduate students.

More and more authors today have begun to focus on diversity at the college level. Some use case studies and student stories to illustrate their points, like Anthony Jack's recent 2019 book *The Privileged Poor: How Elite Colleges Are Failing Disadvantaged Students,*[1] while others take a detailed scholarly history approach like *Stamped from the Beginning* by Ibram Kendi (2016).[2] Our book is unique in that it is co-authored and organized by administrators and instructors, but mostly by recent students from two highly diverse public research universities.[3] Those of us who have shared stories are recent students (Poy, Eager, Martinez, Cohen, Buras). These stories highlight the challenges we faced because of the identity location from which we came: experiences both personal and universal. We also explore the opportunities that we were given that helped us to be successful and which we feel universities can replicate to support their students. To blend the case study and historical analysis approaches, we have provided some background research from the social sciences to understand the driving forces behind our experiences and clarify some evidence-based recommendations for universities to improve their practice. Others of us who organized the book (Stellar, Eggan, Martinez [again], Weiser) processed these stories, and worked to draw out themes and takeaways that can be used to inform the work of colleges and universities. This makes our little book a unique and truly collective work - one that is largely written by the very people about whom we are writing, both those who are most affected and those who have the social power to make change as we see today with the recent Black Lives Matter[4] movement.

Two additional threads weave through the discussion in this book. The first thread draws on scientific evidence to highlight how our conscious decisions as humans are influenced by unconscious decision-making processes. These processes reemerge throughout the stories that we have shared. The evidence for unconscious decision-making, in general, is based in part on the psychology of decision-making and on behavioral neuroscience from brain activity scanning. Together, these studies have sparked interesting new fields, such as neuroeconomics. The other part of that evidence comes from social science research that grows out of a new view of evolution where the group is essential to the thriving of the individual. This evolutionary framing has spawned new areas of research, including positive psychology, investigations of empathy, and more. The combined field is often called "social neuroscience." These exciting new fields build on the traditions of thinking and writing of philosophers and observers throughout history and underlie key concepts in this book as illustrated through our stories, including implicit bias or stereotype threat.

The second additional thread in this book comes from a recognition that, each one of us found our turning point in a learning experience that happened outside of the college classroom, or in a non-traditional experientially driven classroom environment. There is a growing recognition in higher education that experiential education activities, like internships or study abroad programs, can make a valuable complementary contribution to a student's growth based on a traditional academic curriculum of accredited courses and degrees. This experiential approach is not entirely new (it has a long history going back to the ancient practice of learning through apprenticeships in guilds), but what drives it today is the modern view that this kind of applied learning helps students to grow as individuals, develop process skills like critical thinking and teamwork, and get a head start on the skills needed to enter into a career. We hold that this "learning by doing" approach has an even greater impact on students for whom the traditional learning environment was not designed, including first-generation students and historically underrepresented minorities, as it can work against negative influences like stereotype threat and implicit bias. We further believe that these environments provide greater opportunities to enhance student understanding of diversity, and it is a way for colleges and universities to act collaboratively *with* – not *on* – their diverse student populations to improve the student experience and student outcomes.

We have written this book to be read by anyone who is interested in these topics, and we expect no background expertise from the reader. Outside of our individual and shared lived experience, we are not academic experts in the diversity field. We hope the book will be read by current college students, faculty, and administrators, those working in the higher education industry, and anyone else who is interested in college student body diversity and reform of our higher education system. We hope our collective effort helps you as readers to better understand our experience. Ideally, our readers will come away inspired to help to bring about a higher education system that better serves its increasingly diverse student population.

We hope you enjoy reading this book as much as we enjoyed putting it together. Perhaps more than any other force in America today, students – and the universities that support their growth and learning – are molding our future. We must take that force seriously, and we hope this book helps us all to do that with greater understanding and awareness.

CHAPTER 1

INTRODUCTION AND OVERVIEW

We were guided by several beliefs and principles in writing this book that we would like to share with you. We hope that you will keep these principles in mind as you read and carry them forward in your life and work.

First, we believe that words matter. The job of words is to carry messages and ideas, and the subtle differences in the words we choose create powerful results in what we are communicating to others and reaffirming to ourselves. We have endeavored to be thoughtful in our word choices, and we hope you will, too.

Second, we believe that everyone is an expert in their own experience, and those closest to a problem often have the best solutions. This is the reason that we chose to co-author the book in this way, and why we opted to use our own personal stories to investigate and illustrate the experience of minority students in a university environment. If you want to know a student's experience, ask them. If you want to make their experience better or fairer, ask them how.

Third, we believe that we all have work to do in confronting our biases and prejudices – more than we can know – and that it is our responsibility to engage actively in that learning and growth. We learned both about ourselves and about each other in writing this book. We have made intentional efforts to be inclusive and avoid reinforcing biases in our writing, but none of us is perfect. We hope you will be patient with us where we could have done better, and that you will join us in always learning and working to improve.

Fourth, we believe that experiential learning helps to create a more equitable and inclusive learning experience and results in better understanding and openness in a diverse society. The traditional system of education, especially higher education, was designed for a homogenous and elite populous and is known to reward certain groups over others. Today, from our direct, personal experiences, we believe that applied learning experiences allowed us to understand ourselves and others, and helped us to see our place within a higher education environment more easily than traditional classroom settings.

Fifth, and finally, we believe that supporting diversity and inclusion in higher educational institutions is a moral imperative and that a diverse student body is a great asset to their institutions and all students who attend them, especially now. Simply accepting students from diverse backgrounds is not enough – the institutions must be designed to create learning environments that serve all of their students, provide opportunities for learning about diversity and practicing inclusion, and appreciate the richness that diversity brings to the campus.

WORDS MATTER

There is a way of speaking that puts a person first.

Think about it when you see someone who is homeless. You could say, "There is a person who is homeless," or you could say, "There is a homeless person." What is the difference and why would you choose one way of speaking over the other? The answer is that the first way opens the possibility for change, invites the thought that the person was not always homeless, and produces less of an us-versus-them distinction. The implication, of course, is that with some slight change in health, employment, or other status, you could well be the person who is now homeless.

The distinction above seems subtle. But the brain is built to form distinctions that divide people into in-groups and out-groups.[5] Our brains do this automatically, often without conscious awareness. The fact that a judgment may be unconscious does not mean it is unimportant. One example of an unconscious judgment with a serious practical result is demonstrated in a job placement study[6] that showed a marked decrease in call-back rate when a black-sounding name was placed at the top of a resume versus when a white-sounding name was on exactly the same resume.

Studies[7] investigating the ways in which babies react to the speech of strangers reveal how judgments of in-group and out-group may be both basic to our nature and unconscious. Before babies say actual words, they start to babble selectively in the sounds of the language that they hear around them and stop making the random sounds of all possible languages. While that observation may not be surprising in itself, a key observation is that if a baby hears a non-native speaker at this stage, it shows a small reaction that it does not show to a similarly unfamiliar voice speaking words in its own language. This baby has clearly grouped humans into in-groups and out-groups based on language sounds even before learning to speak. We assume the baby is not aware of this decision. It turns out that typically neither are we when we make similar groupings as adults.

The words that we choose also can veer into the category of microaggressions. "Micro" references a seemingly small or perhaps innocent display, like the terms we use, how we choose to speak, the jokes we make, and the compliments we give. The term "microaggression" was popularized by researcher Derald Sue,[8] who famously wrote about how people complimented him as an Asian whose English was very good, even though he was born in the United States and English is his native language. People have powerful attachments to their gender, ethnic, racial, and other identities.

While the display may be unconscious or invisible to any single speaker, due to cultural asymmetry and frequent occurrence, the cumulative effect of microaggressions becomes a burden on the receiver. Microaggressions highlight the pain and discomfort stemming from stereotypes that are often connected with or result in being disadvantaged.

In a college environment, with a majority culture, minority students may seek respite from these microaggressions in groups that match their own identity. Certainly, college campuses are replete with groups that celebrate the commonality of identity groups, both small-scale and involved in the establishment of social movements like #BlackLivesMatter and #MeToo on Twitter. We believe that by connecting college students across social and identity groups in honest, supportive conversations, colleges and universities can and should encourage deeper felt-knowledge understanding of these important issues.

All stereotype-influenced actions, even if they are unintentional, and maybe especially if they are unnoticed, reduce the optimism and strength needed for our students to face a complex world with its uncertainties. A college experience within a diverse student body provides an opportunity to encourage positive social dynamics and deepen intellectual understanding, not just in the classroom, but in interpersonal experience. That brings us back to the power of the group. When the group is not supportive, and/or when it is the majority culture and you are not a part of it, stereotype threat, self-handicapping, and the pernicious undermining of microaggressions can take a continuing toll on students and their success in college and afterward.

Words matter because thinking matters, and we largely formulate our thoughts in words. Truly listening to our own words offers an unmatched entry point into the subconscious workings of our brains. Words set the tone for our unconscious processing of implicit biases, in-group/out-group distinctions, and so much more. If there is ever a hope of sorting out our feelings on an issue we care deeply about, we very often have to begin by getting the words right. The undergraduate experience is an ideal time for us all to begin to learn how we think and start to develop our ability to express our thoughts in a diverse modern world. If you are in a position to create any programs, organizations, or initiatives, we hope that you will include those who you seek to serve in their creation, as they are likely to be true experts.

WE ALL HAVE WORK TO DO – MORE THAN WE CAN KNOW: UNDERSTANDING THE UNCONSCIOUS DECISION-MAKING BUILT INTO OUR BRAINS AND EVOLVING PAST IMPLICIT EXPECTATIONS

We all naturally carry the illusion that we are exactly the thinking, speaking person that we consciously experience. Philosophers and scientists have known for a long time that there is more to us than that - we make many decisions based on emotional and unconscious processes. Today, modern neuroscience's growing understanding of how the brain functions reinforces this conclusion. In our day-to-day life, we apply unconscious principles to how we interact as people from different origins even without knowing it. Where does this unconscious decision-making come from in our brains, how does it get into our behavior (possibly without the conscious "us" knowing about it), and what ultimately is the role of society in shaping the unconscious brain's influence?

The brain is built so that most simple functions, like reflexes, are handled at the lower parts of the brain that are typically evolutionarily older. We are simply unaware of how they operate. For example, none of us, not even a neurologist, can explain exactly how we perform the seemingly simple task of walking. At least, we could not explain it in the same way that all of us could explain how to make a chocolate cake from our grandmother's favorite recipe. With normal walking on a nice, dry, solid surface, the computational process inside our nervous system handles the legs, feet, coordination, balance, and other necessary processes. Whatever most of us learned about how to walk, we learned long ago and stored it somewhere deep in our brain outside of conscious awareness. This is both completely normal as well as useful, as it allows us to concentrate on other things like where we want to go, and not be "too dumb to walk and chew gum at the same time," as the old saying goes. On the other hand, this unconscious awareness can also cause problems, for example, if we have acquired the habit of a limp from a long-healed injury – although the source of this behavior may be long gone, our unconscious muscle memory continues to negatively influence our gait.

Even in very high-level, sophisticated decisions, ranging from the choice of a college major to the choice of a friend or even life-partner, we still see the influence of a second hidden decision-maker. This influence is particularly strong in social interactions involving trust. Let us consider an example involving deception.[9] In a fascinating experiment, people were asked to record video statements that they knew were either true or false. The experimenters then filtered the audio part of the recording so that the listener could not make out the actual words but could hear the tone and pace of the speech and could see the facial expressions of the speaker. When these videos were shown to other subjects, they could tell most of the time which person was lying. The nonverbal communication leaked the truth through even without words.

This unconscious decision-making extends far past our individual actions and interpersonal interactions into other decisions about our economy and our society. In 2002, Princeton University psychologist Daniel Kahneman, who studies decision-making, won the Nobel Prize in the field of Economics, and in 2011, he wrote a book, *Thinking, Fast and Slow*,[10] showing how we use short-cut heuristics to make important decisions, like purchases in the stock market. The research work he and others did started a field called "behavioral economics" that has had broad implications for other fields, including business leadership and marketing, e.g. *Start with Why*[11] or *Likeconomics*.[12]

In 2011, the brain-scanning neuroscientist David Eagleman published a book central to this discussion: *Incognito: The Secret Lives of the Hidden Brain*.[13] Eagleman's book does make the point that we are often unaware of hidden influences and while many of them are innocent, like learning the route home so you can practically walk it in your sleep; some are not, like the lower call-back rate already mentioned when a black-sounding name is at the top of the job applicant's resume. Unconscious or "incognito" decision-making processes are everywhere and have varying levels of impact on our colleges and universities, particularly with historically underrepresented and underserved student populations.

With this understanding of our incognito processing, we feel it is important for all of us to do what we can to examine and address the assumptions, prejudices, and biases that are guiding our actions or decisions because these have a real influence on others' experience and quality of life. Especially for those in a position of power or authority, and even more so, for those who belong to historically privileged groups, it is important to make visible this hidden thinking if we are truly to create more just and equitable institutions. For example, even our best efforts at equalizing success outcomes for our students are often based on assumptions of student deficits – we believe the students that are less successful are not as capable (even if by no fault of their own), so our interventions must be focused on helping the student to improve their skills and abilities. While this may be part of the story, that causes us to dismiss the possibility that our *institutions* are deficient, for example, by not properly rewarding all forms of student talent, or ignoring the fact that we are assuming prior knowledge about the systems or structures that have nothing to do with the content of what we are teaching or testing.

For example, if a professor assumes that a student went to bad primary and secondary schools, they might expect that they are not prepared to be successful in their class. If that student struggles, they may be less likely to reach out and see what the problem might be or take ownership over the results. But maybe that student is perfectly capable academically but is the first in their family to go to college, lacking anyone to help them understand how college classes are set up. Maybe they have never heard the word "syllabus" and do not understand where to find assignments, and so they continue to struggle. They themselves may have come with self-limiting biases, and so do not believe they have the right to ask questions or request extra help. Surely, the learning objectives that we are testing in university are not meant to be defined by whether a student knows the word "syllabus" – so we may need to change *our* practices and beliefs, to be better able to provide an equitable experience that gives every student a chance to succeed and fairly tests their relevant knowledge and abilities. But we cannot discover that unless we first examine the assumptions that are driving those practices.

Recall the previous example of the unconscious limp that persists even though the injury that caused it has long since healed. If we want to fix the limp, we must first be aware of that limp, and then make conscious the unconscious process of walking, in order to begin the hard work of reforming those habits and adjusting our muscle memory. In the same way, if we are to begin the process of reducing the impact of prejudice or bias on our behaviors and choices, we must first acknowledge those mental habits, explicitly examine the assumptions in our thinking, and then begin the hard work of changing them.

The example of the limp is an apt one, because just as the limp came from an injury that has since healed, many of our unconscious decision-making processes may have come from survival instincts that are no longer useful. Evolution shaped our brains and behaviors by selecting genes for certain adaptive traits that promoted survival, and we sometimes refer to this selection as an example of "the selfish gene" process where the genes use an organism to promote their own survival. In the biological family, it makes genetic computational sense to sacrifice yourself if it were for two or more of your siblings, since they each share half your genes. From the gene's perspective, that would be the same as you surviving.

So why do we have any biological tendencies toward altruism, sacrificing ourselves for the good of individuals even outside our immediate family, who do not share our genes? The answer is that more recent thinking about evolution has discovered something else from early human evolutionary history – the power of the social group or tribe in helping the individual survive. We see evidence of brain mechanisms that promote group functioning beyond the biological family, essential for how we relate to each other as part of our in-group or out-group.

A classic example is the hormone oxytocin, which, according to researchers, including behavioral economist Paul Zak,[14] can produce trust between humans. Oxytocin was first known by pediatricians to produce the reflex of milk let-down in a mother's breast associated with nursing. Scientists now believe that oxytocin contributes to a mother's social bond with her baby, in both humans and other mammals.[15] More recently, social neuroscience researchers have shown that oxytocin increases trust between all identified in-group members, across ages and genders. In neuroeconomics games involving money, used to investigate social psychology concepts, there is greater monetary sharing behavior if the participants are first given an oxytocin treatment. The change in behavior is also reflected in differences in brain scans. Even more interesting is that oxytocin may be best released in another human by giving them a welcome hug.[16]

We would call this bonding; however, it is not quite that simple. The same way oxytocin seems to increase in-group sharing, it also seems to decrease out-group sharing. This makes some sense, as groups of humans living near each other early in human evolution would likely be in competition for the same scarce resources. Strengthening the in-group bond seems naturally to lead to greater conflict with the out-group.[17] This kind of tribalism pits various groups against each other: white against black, rich against poor, light-skinned against darker-skinned. Much has been written about tribalism, e.g. *The Righteous Mind: Why Good People are Divided by Politics and Religion,*[18] and much has been written about discrimination within and between groups, e.g. *Race and Colorism in Education.*[19]

Although one result is problematic tribalism, oxytocin also explains how we develop and experience compassion for others. A great deal is written today about empathy and how it is triggered,[20] especially when evoked by the experience of one individual. For this reason, some children's charities have found that it is useful to put the face and story of an individual child on the screen and ask the audience to contribute to that child (or one just like them). We feel for the individual, where we may not feel for the group. Perhaps that is why we chose in this book the format of five stories.

In the late 1970s, psychologist David Premack coined a term, "Theory of Mind," that says we humans are really built to try to figure out what another human wants.[21] We automatically seek to figure out the goal or purpose of another person's actions. Now, neuroscientists think that this drive to understand each other's motivations may be hard-wired in our brains. We have long known that our brains contain neurons in our motor command and control systems that fire to produce a movement, like picking up a peanut and putting it in our mouths. What we have learned more recently, first in non-human primates, is that these same motor neurons may also fire when we see someone else do that action. We call the neurons that sympathetically fire "mirror neurons."[22] This idea has been extended to empathy. When we see that someone is in pain, frustrated, disadvantaged, or denied from getting what they want, we feel it too. Our brains automatically can put us in their place, mirroring their neurons. But do we actually act with compassion and do something to help? Do college students act to help others or do they simply watch and study the problem?

ROLE OF EXPERIENTIAL EDUCATION

Empathy is a powerful tool to reduce the tribalism that seems to be a part of our shared humanity. When people are interacting, making eye contact, observing each other's pain and triumphs, and working together toward shared goals, empathy has room to grow. Experiential education activities like these foster empathy in a way that traditional classroom education may not. If the students who are engaging in that experiential learning come from diverse backgrounds, empathy develops across the lines of in-groups and out-groups of ethnicity, socioeconomic status, gender identity, or country of origin.

Experiential education can also help reduce the influence of some of the biases in our higher education system that we discussed earlier. Direct experiences interacting experientially with others allows students to see others as whole people. Experiential learning in a diverse environment benefits the instructor, as well, who learns to develop the understanding needed to more fully support and engage their students. Although societal prejudices and biases are certain to pervade college experiential learning environments, properly developed experiential learning activities can reduce prejudiced practices of both the students and those responsible for their education. Experiential education frees higher education of the ivory-tower isolation in a monastery-like environment where cloistered faculty and students meet over classes and lectures to transfer knowledge.

One of the most intense forms of experiential education is a work-based method called cooperative education. While the concept of apprenticeship goes back 1,500 years to the labor guilds, it was not until 1906 that an engineering professor at the University of Cincinnati, Herman Schneider, brought the concept of cooperative education to higher education.[23] In Schneider's cooperative education program, engineering students alternated periods of full-time work in the industry with periods of full-time study at the university.[24] The model was adopted by a few other universities and colleges, including Northeastern, Drexel, and Antioch, before developing across the country, and soon, around the world.

Today, we might call that cooperative education work experience an internship, like the part-time and unpaid internships that students are familiar with. Experiential learning activities in higher education include internships, as well study abroad, undergraduate research, and service-learning, and more. Most universities and colleges (correctly) feel they must offer these kinds of curriculum-complementing activities to attract and retain good students. A new trend is to document them through digital badges, skills-based resumes, or entries into what is called the "co-curricular transcript."[25] Companies also like to see activities that suggest a job candidate is developing the soft skills necessary to work in a company to complement the facts-and-theories knowledge gained in a classroom. More recently, this combination has been referred to as T-shaped skills,[26] where the vertical part of the T signifies deep disciplinary knowledge, and the top of the T represents the broader skills that enable people to collaborate across disciplines and with diverse groups of people. Employers highly value these traits and actively search for skills like communication and the ability to work in teams.

Learning from experience channels both the brain's conscious and unconscious processes.[27] This kind of learning can powerfully complement a classic academic curriculum to produce a more mature and work-ready student, as well as open opportunities for empathy, relationship building, and deep learning. Furthermore, it is useful to keep this brain-based, unconscious decision-making process in mind when considering how best to optimize students' ability to learn from one another in a diverse population during their college years. Rather than exclusively provide courses, lectures, and policies that discuss diversity, we can do more learning *from one another* through engaging experiences.

DIVERSITY IN HIGHER EDUCATION AS BOTH A MORAL IMPERATIVE AND GREAT ASSET TO THE INSTITUTIONS AND ALL STUDENTS THAT THEY SERVE

The United States is changing and becoming more diverse, a shift that is apparent on our college campuses. Over the last few decades, many colleges and universities have made commitments to address diversity and even built values of inclusion into their student enrollment plans. While the mission is honorable, we have noticed a lack of the fine-grained student-based cultural understanding needed to better accommodate this new diverse student body and create a harmonious campus. As Anthony Jack points out in his book, cited in the Preface, many of the student stories go unspoken.

A drive for harmony has been said to be a characteristic of the human race, and some authors have argued that we are, in fact, getting better, pointing out for example that society's murder rate has declined markedly over the centuries.[28] On a more relevant level, it is clear that having diversity is good for business leading to better problem-solving.[29] It is perhaps, then, not surprising that diversity is often featured prominently in a college or university's strategic plan as they try to educate their students to be better future citizens and productively contribute to a harmonious world.

Thinking, talking about, and acting on issues of diversity brings one quickly to the working world. We recognize that many global businesses and professions require college graduates to work with diverse groups of people, domestically and internationally. On the campus itself, a commitment to welcoming all people naturally promotes enhanced graduation rates, which is key to both student and institutional success. We recognize that many people have strong feelings about this topic. We understand that people have a natural tendency to feel more comfortable within our "tribes." But we also recognize that society must do better than it has done in the past to increase opportunities for growth for all people.

E Pluribus Unum: "out of many, one." To become one country, we must leverage our diversity and balance our tribalism. College is a good place to practice building inclusive communities.

OUR STORIES

In this book, we have shared our stories: five of them, to be exact. We use each story to illustrate how experiences in college, often outside the classroom, can be used to explore and understand the implications of increasing college student diversity. These personal stories also have a powerful way of connecting with the hidden processes in our brains. Our belief is that when unconscious decision-making processes are well integrated with conscious decision-making processes based on academic facts and theories, higher education can have a high impact on diversity understanding. We are all blessedly different, but we are all built from the same gene pool with the same basic brain structure, giving rise to commonalities in how we think and operate that allow for mutual understanding of others' emotions, experiences, fears, and desires.

We hope that by sharing through stories that you as a reader can connect more personally with our life experiences – even if the precise details of our experiences differ from your own. We also hope that these experiences help to contextualize and make relevant the social science that we are sharing, with the goal of galvanizing a commitment to improving our institutions. We are not just talking about data, brain science, and best practices. We are talking about people, their lives, and their experiences; experiences that in many ways mirror ours.

Each of these stories will illustrate a key social neuroscience principle. Since the stories come from our college experiences, they contain ideas about what colleges and universities might do to address the issues of students on their campuses. The storytellers want to help students and institutions craft student experiences that will prove more successful in the construction of a harmonious campus. These stories will support a diverse campus in a diverse world, where students will work in cross-cultural, cross-functional teams after graduation. We think it is best for the students to pick up these skills while in college, rather than afterward, when a job may be on the line. Employers we know say the same. They want our students to be able to team up across socio-cultural and national borders in order to share their knowledge and problem-solve together.

CHAPTER 2: *Philosophy: A field of white men with white beards pondering white people problems*
BENY'S STORY | Implicit Bias

College is by nature an uncomfortable new experience. But for those students who do not have the appearance or history of the majority culture, the discomfort can be a struggle indeed. Beny was excited for his college experience to begin, but as a Latino on a campus of mostly white faculty in upstate New York, he began to face challenges that he never expected. Few people, and perhaps even fewer professors, claim to be racist, but psychologists believe that we all innately exhibit implicit racially-biased tendencies. While research continues on this issue, what can be done in the present moment? This chapter follows Beny's unusual work throughout his college career on the issue of diversification of faculty and on the importance of him finding a mentor of a similar background to his own through an internship.

CHAPTER 3: *Women in Science*
RACHEL'S STORY | Self-handicapping

While Rachel was working an internship at a hospital during high school, a nurse with the best of intentions offered her some advice: "Be a nurse, marry a doctor." It was such a short phrase, with nothing truly meant by it, but it stuck within Rachel's deep unconscious mind. As a result, she began to self-handicap, a process by which individuals of all ages and professions intentionally or unintentionally avoid situations where they may perform poorly. Rachel's story describes how she found help overcoming this challenge via experiential learning opportunities.

CHAPTER 4: *Defying Gravity*

CHRISEL'S STORY | Low Socioeconomic Status and Peer Support

Chrisel Martinez tells a compelling story of her childhood in Harlem and being raised by a single mother with many siblings. With the help of her mother's strong will and commitment to higher education, Chrisel navigated her circumstances and was admitted to college, setting a new standard for her and her family. However, she needed some help. The Educational Opportunity Program (EOP) at the University at Albany provided that help with a disciplined new family of peers - a home away from home. Chrisel's story explores the power of groups that can elevate individual students through conscious and unconscious bonding.

CHAPTER 5: *Find Your Niche*

MARC'S STORY | In-group/Out-group

Because humans are naturally social creatures, groups form quickly in college that often trace back to common interests and friends from high school. Growing up in a small town nestled in Jewish culture before moving away to a large, diverse college presented a challenge for Marc: How to make it from the out-group to the in-group? This chapter follows Marc's journey down multiple avenues in an effort to accomplish his goal, but ultimately arrives at his achievement of becoming a student leader of the entire SUNY student government system.

CHAPTER 6: *The Fear of Starting Over*
AGATA'S STORY | Stereotype Threat

As a first-generation Polish immigrant student, Agata expected a traditional college experience where she would sit in the back of the class, do her work alone, and hope not to be called on because English was her second language. This plan changed when Agata had a non-traditional classroom experience that seemed to recognize that different students absorb, process, comprehend, and recite information differently. This chapter follows Agata's ongoing college journey and explores the impact of stereotype threat, where a student's self-perception of their identity can lead to underperformance, and how she overcame it to find her success.

Now, it's time to start telling stories that illustrate the social neuroscience concepts that we have introduced. Through narratives, we will surface suggestions for how higher education could use experiential learning to better serve its increasingly diverse college student populations. At the end of the book, in a concluding chapter, we will return to summarize conclusions on the issue of institutional improvement.

CHAPTER 2

BENY'S STORY:

IMPLICIT BIAS

Philosophy: A field of white men with
white beards pondering white people problems

Growing up in the Bronx is tough, but you get used to it …
and you become proud of it. In the Bronx, we all suffer from the
same condition: "the struggle." If and when you survive, you
become an elite member within an elite community known as the
"Bronxites." We recognize each other through the not-very-discreet
"X" formation we make with our arms when our hometown is
mentioned. Our stern faces should not necessarily be taken as
indicators of how we feel inside: our expressions are a tribute to
the history of our mean and untrusting streets. Our communities
are beyond diverse and we all relish in each other's cultures because,
really, we have no choice when the music penetrates the thin walls
of our tattered apartments.

The Bronx was once burning, but it rose from the ashes like a phoenix, dusting off the remains of impotent politicians. Building owners were paying off gang members to burn their buildings down for the insurance money, sometimes with people in them who had no other place to go. The streets were littered with crime, gang violence, and garbage. President Jimmy Carter visited the Bronx in 1977 to point out the realities of government inaction, but still didn't do anything to significantly improve it.[30] This is a major part of our history and it remains in the back of our minds – in the back of my mind – when we think about the Bronx. It, directly and indirectly, forms part of the base of our identities.

I would be lying if I said that all the issues that existed in 1977 do not still exist today, but we're getting better.[31] As you can see, it's not easy, and I won't pretend that I didn't wish that it was better, but the Bronx is my home. The adversities that I, and many others like myself, face make us who we are and who we aspire to be.

Just a few short years ago, I was a high school senior shopping for the university that best fit me at the time. I knew that I didn't want to stay home. I knew that I didn't want to be too far from home. I knew that I didn't want to pay too much, and most importantly I knew that I wanted to be on a diverse campus with peers who could understand my perspective. I wanted to live on a campus with people who understood and appreciated the challenges that I have faced in my life and would not be quick to judge me by the stern expression on my face.

Unfortunately, I looked to my left and I looked to my right and realized the grim truth about growing up in the Bronx. Many of my hometown friends either had few to no collegiate aspirations or would not dream of it because of the hardships they had faced in their lives. Sadly, many of them did not believe they deserved it. When I was admitted to the University at Albany, I accepted that the chances of meeting people like me were slim. Still, I was determined to be different from what I thought would be the people in my new environment.

The opposite happened. To my surprise, I entered the University at Albany surrounded by an expanded family who shared my experiences. By that I mean specifically that I was admitted into the university as a student in my college's Educational Opportunities Program (EOP).[32] I found out that I would have the privilege of attending an intensive, five-week summer pre-freshman year orientation program with a new tough-love group of people who quickly transitioned from my peers to my family. This summer program, or "boot camp" as we liked to call it, immersed me in a new environment and taught me the skills that were needed to survive in college. But, most importantly, it taught us all how to do it together, building in us a group survival mentality like we were the US Marines, like we were all from the Bronx. The EOP at the University at Albany is made up of all types of underrepresented and underprivileged students, established in 1968 as a direct result of the Civil Rights movement. It thrives on the philosophy that economics strongly impacts the academics of the underprivileged, but that they are still very capable and brilliant students. It operates on the principle that in being together and supporting each other, we can do great and unexpected things.

The summer program was not easy, but it got me through my years at the University at Albany. I can look back confidently and say that much of my success can be attributed to those first five weeks. Because of that summer, we do more than just "survive." In fact, we do better than the rest of the students, with retention and graduation rates higher than the campus average. I can talk endlessly about EOP, but that's not all that this chapter is about – so here I'll pivot to other ways diversity affected my university life.

HOW I CHAMPIONED THE ISSUE OF FACULTY DIVERSITY

After my first few years in college, I found myself asking very different questions from my high school days, especially as I contemplated furthering my education beyond a bachelor's degree. As a high school senior, I thought about my peers and the importance of their diversity. Then, as I settled into comfort within their differences, I found myself fighting a different and much more difficult battle. Diversity is an issue that is plaguing the nation and has its roots firmly planted in historical inequities. At the level of university faculty, lack of diversity is even more entrenched than in the student body.

This issue dawned on me when I first became a member of my university's Student Association. As a Student Senator, I had my own constituency of over 1,500 students. I ran a tough campaign and made sure that my constituency knew who I was and that I was available to advocate on their behalf. Out of the many issues that were communicated to me, the one that stood out to me the most was the issue of faculty diversity. A constituent of Latino descent told me that the professors didn't look like him and he didn't even feel like his professors understood him. His feeling of alienation resonated deeply with me when I reflected on my own department, the Department of Philosophy.

The step that finally prompted me to look deeper was when I took note of just how many professors of color there were in my major: at the time of my undergraduate studies, a total of one. That one philosophy professor, however, quickly and intentionally became my mentor and academic advisor. I had wanted someone who could understand me and guide me through the experience of being the minority in the room. As I delved deeper into my major, I started seeing fewer and fewer of not only Latino or Black students, but women as well in my classrooms.

After these realizations, I began to understand my own gnawing sense of non-belonging from my earlier years in college. There were few to no students that looked like me in my major. There was one "diverse" faculty member, and even their curriculum was saturated with studying the works of privileged white males.

Philosophy, the king of all the humanities, is supposed to be inclusive of all ideologies and perspectives. Sadly, though, it has historically been a field for the privileged; that is, white men with white beards and white hair. That is the stereotype of the philosopher and, unfortunately for me, I hardly fit that description.

ONE ACTION I TOOK TO PROMOTE THE DIVERSITY OF THE FACULTY DIVERSITY

Through the student government, I became close with several senior academic administrators. Together, we decided that it was important to create a conversation on the perspectives of students and professors on the status of our faculty diversity. I wanted to understand the challenges of hiring faculty from diverse backgrounds. I particularly wanted the faculty and administration to hear what it means to our students to have nearly 35% Black and Latino students, but fewer than 10% Black and Latino faculty. (Side Bar: It is important to note that, of that 10%, some were professors from abroad that fell into those categories. This helped to bolster their appearance of being diverse. While all diversity is important, it is even more important that we prioritize those that came from and lived in historically disadvantaged communities.)

After much planning, one afternoon in the fall, we convened about 150 students over coffee and cookies, including many representatives from the student government and approximately 50 faculty members who served on faculty search committees. We had a brief presentation on the history of the university's growing student diversity and stagnant faculty diversity. Our university diversity officer set the stage with introductory remarks, and a few students shared their experiences, including myself. Then, in groups of about ten people, we held a round-table discussion of students and faculty followed by a whole group sharing session. My initial impression of that evening was that everyone, especially faculty, was aware of the issue and the benefits of resolving it, but struggled with the logistics - in other words, the politics - of making progress happen.

The faculty made reasonable points about the competitive nature of hiring a diverse faculty member and the continuing struggle for resources, particularly in a public university that is also committed to maintaining an affordable tuition (for which I am grateful). They also made the standard argument about excellence and the challenge of hiring the very best faculty as scholars and teachers, so as to be the very best university possible. I am dubious of this argument, as I think the diverse faculty are out there even if it is competitive to hire them. In addition, how successful can we truly be when we have not exposed students to the realities of a world that is diverse and only growing? After all, the university is recruiting diverse students. How about, for example, establishing a program to track a few of those students into teaching positions, creating opportunities for them to stay at the university as professors later on? Other universities have taken this approach, establishing such "pipeline programs."[33] Even if the program did not yield big numbers, it would be symbolically significant in that everyone could see the university was trying, not making excuses. Also, in my experience, even if just one faculty member is hired as a result of a pipeline program, they often become mentors to students - even those outside of their own department. At the end of the day, while the dialogue did not directly inspire any immediate policy changes, it did spark the development of a series called "Conversations for Change" that still occurs today and invites scholars of diversity in higher education and broader society to speak.

MY CRUCIAL INTERNSHIP EXPERIENCE

While I first loved philosophy for its intrinsic acceptance for all thought and ideas, I found out that I had more in common with politics. Politics embraced me. When I looked at it, I saw something familiar that reminded me of who I was, something that empowered my identity. All in all, philosophy, at the time, seemed to be a field for white men with white hair that pondered and mused about white people problems. When I walked down the street in my neighborhood in the Bronx my people didn't seem to be pondering the nature of their existence - at least not in those exact terms. They were, in fact, a bit more concerned about whether the decisions they made today would help them exist until tomorrow.

Spending those semesters advocating for the representation of minorities in faculty lit a flame in me. I was excited by the departmental and administrative politics involved in making the decision to fund programs that work to diversify faculty. The summer prior, I had the privilege to intern in the Manhattan office of New York State Assembly Speaker Carl E. Heastie, to whom I was previously introduced while I was studying abroad in Cuba. Needless to say, when I met him again, we had a good conversation - before I asked him for a job. That summer, I served as a Research Assistant in the Speaker's office, an office that constantly featured various leaders of the state.

This opportunity, afforded to me by the kindness of the first Black Speaker of the New York State Assembly, made all the difference. Not only because of the value of the opportunity, but because he understood "the struggle," being from the Bronx himself and having fervently supported funding EOP programs as a legislative leader. Importantly, he was able to make my internship a paid opportunity. This might not seem like a big deal to many, but even though I had all the passion and hunger to pursue the experience,

I could not afford the simple commute to his office. That is the difference between someone (e.g. a professor, a boss) who simply offers the value of an experience and someone who goes the extra mile to make it possible for you to have the experience. It is crucial to also understand that providing the means to make this life-changing opportunity possible must not be perceived as an act of charity. Instead, it should be perceived as a clear necessity. To cross over from charity to collaboration, someone has to try and understand my "struggle."

LESSONS FROM SOCIAL SCIENCE ABOUT IMPLICIT BIAS AND WHY FACULTY DIVERSITY MATTERS

Implicit bias is what it sounds like: it is a bias we carry around with us and of which we are unaware. This phenomenon was revealed about two decades ago by the implicit bias test developed and presented by two social psychology researchers, Banaji and Greenwald,[34] prompting a new body of research.[35] To detect implicit bias between white and black racial groups, the test goes something like this. First, the subject is trained to rapidly react to a series of words appearing on a computer screen classifying them as either positive or negative (e.g. courageous, conniving) by pressing a specific computer key either on the left or the right of the keyboard. The reaction time is measured. The same is done with black versus white faces. Then, a second condition is established where the subject must make two simultaneous judgments: 1) determining if a word is in the positive or negative category and

2) determining if a face is white or black. Making two judgments at once is a more complex decision task and takes more mental computation, so the reaction time is naturally a bit slower.

The key to this study is comparing the reaction times when positive words are associated with black versus white faces. When positive words are associated with black faces rather than white faces, reaction time is longest. It is as though associating black faces with positive words is harder, requiring more mental computation, and hence results in a longer reaction time. It is precisely this longer reaction time that revealed what came to be known as *implicit bias*. A fascinating takeaway from the study was that most people who took the test showed the reaction time bias *and* were unaware of it. As a result, the implicit bias test has generated much interest in unconscious decision-making, and that topic has appeared in many popular books, e.g. Malcolm Gladwell's *Blink*[36] or Shankar Vedantam's *The Hidden Brain*.[37]

Like many dramatic findings, subsequent research has given us context on the limitations on test result interpretation. For example, as written about recently in *The Cut* for a public audience, some problems have emerged with the test itself.[38] For example, the reaction time measure of implicit bias has been shown to increase if the test itself is conducted in a noisy room. While the noise could make it harder to concentrate on the task, no one believes that raising the noise level increases someone's implicit bias. Another example is that implicit bias retests do not give quite the same results as the first test. For example, if the test was given twice to ten people, and after each test the participants were asked to line up in order of bias, one would expect the order of the results to be roughly the same. The order would be the same with a simple objective measure like height or weight. With implicit bias test results, however, only about half of the people stand in the exact same order as they did in the first run of the test. While that result does suggest some caution, particularly in the interpretation of an individual case, it does not invalidate the test. There is something there, nevertheless.

To return to my story, the lesson here is that we are always factoring in the social context of a situation, even if we are not aware of it. This applies to the first impression students have when they look at the professor in the front of the classroom. It is true, of course, that an excellent professor can offer a positive interpersonal relationship to any student of any background in addition to being the classic dispenser of classroom knowledge. But seeing yourself in the person of the instructor still matters, especially in quantitative classes in STEM fields that are taken during the freshman year.[39] Additional studies reveal that this effect is common in the U.S.[40] and occurs at all levels of education, including high school, when the institution's majority culture is not the student's own.[41] Again, match or mismatch may not be a problem for an individual student-professor interaction where a personal rapport can be established and high expectations and levels of support can be set. But it is a problem for first impressions, large classes, and an unknown number of students like Beny, who experience this pattern of increasing discouragement.

IMPLICIT BIAS AND SOME THOUGHTS ABOUT WHAT HIGHER EDUCATION CAN DO ABOUT IT

So, how does a college or university diversify its faculty? We see the issue as one of intention. If an institution intends to foster diversity, the work starts by putting out that message in the pronouncements of the leadership. Then, it is important to write it down in places where the institution says what it wants to become, like the strategic plan. It could be as simple as Beny's statement that the university wants a faculty that looks more like its students.

If intention is the first step, the second step is to get to the operational searching entity to behave differently. In many places, that entity is the faculty search committee of each academic department. Once they have been given the charge to search for a particular type of scholar the department wants to hire, they have to do more than just post the job advertisement (even if it is in the right journals as indicated by the Diversity Office), vet applications, and invite some folks for an interview. The search committee must also be an active recruiting body that reaches out to all places, e.g. where potential minority faculty might be found. That may mean conferences, certain universities like those which are Historically Black Colleges and Universities, or even tracking its own diverse undergraduates into PhD programs to become faculty in a pipeline program. Search committees will naturally resist the tendency to stray from the highest possible standards of faculty excellence, and that is good. But they must work hard to build an excellent and diverse pool of applicants in the first place.

Finally, in a third and final step, the university or college leadership must support the search committee with resources when it comes up with a candidate. That is to say, because the candidate will be both from an underrepresented identity group and excellent, they will likely be approached by competing institutions as well, and it may simply cost more to attract them. If the leadership is unwilling to commit sufficient resources, the first two steps are undermined.

Another separate, but related question is: how does a college or university hold onto its minority faculty when they are sought after by other institutions? First, there must be a mechanism at the senior administrative level where cases of such faculty raiding can be rapidly evaluated and a counterplan launched with ready resources. Typically, that work involves both the department chair and the dean, but it may require involvement at a higher administrative level. Simply having a robust set of programs already established to promote faculty diversity at the college or university can be very helpful. As the old saying goes, "the best defense may be a good offense."

If the institution is seen trying in many ways to build diversity and inclusion, the administration sets a tone that pays off in recruitment. It also helps to have programs for student recruitment and retention (e.g. the EOP program), clear curriculum features (like diversity courses in general education components), special lectures, workshops, and celebratory events. Additionally, it helps to have pipeline programs and service-learning work in the local community. Some institutions, like the University of Maryland Baltimore County (UMBC),[42] are well known for generating large numbers of minority doctoral degrees in fields like engineering and medicine even though they are smaller institutions than state flagship universities.[43] When resources are dedicated in all of these areas, it creates a tone that makes the institution a welcoming and authentic place, which goes a long way in holding onto diverse faculty. This is what some of the UMBC faculty have told some of us at the University at Albany when they visited.

What can students do to help, respectfully but effectively, to drive the faculty diversity agenda? They can do what they always do. First, show up like Beny did, and second, engage in authentic conversation. It is a matter of sharing good ideas. Second, keep the issue of diverse faculty recruitment at the forefront of the university or college agenda, especially when other issues surface and demand resources. Everyone must pitch in, including students.

CHAPTER 3

RACHEL'S STORY:

SELF-HANDICAPPING

———

Women in Science

I was raised in East Greenbush, a small town on the outskirts of what I saw then as the booming capital of New York, Albany. Ever since I was young, as the elder of two sisters, I felt an obligation to serve as a role model. You know the type: straight-A student, varsity letter awards, et cetera. Luckily for my parents, they had passed on the genes for a strong type-A personality. I've always been one of those people who likes to be ahead of the game, which might include getting a paper done four days before it's due or reading all the novels for English class the first month of school just to be prepared for when we finally got to that point in the curriculum. This story falls right into that trait.

I fell in love with science my junior year of high school. I remember sitting in chemistry class fascinated by the equations, compounds, and experiments. It was the first time I was confident in my ability to do something so complex, and I could not get enough of it. I was early to class every day, sitting in the front row with my hand up, ready to answer anything my teacher would throw at the class.

It was also from a young age that I discovered I loved caring for others and knowing that I was making a difference in the world. From the personal level, taking care of my family when they were sick, to the macro-level of hundreds of hours of community service and volunteer work throughout my teenage years, I always found helping people rewarding. Among my friends, I was known for living by the saying 'go big or go home' and I was set on doing as many big things as one girl could do before I had to be home at night by curfew.

By the time senior year rolled around and I was deciding on colleges and majors, there was no doubt in my mind what I wanted to do. Yes, you guessed it: pre-med! It was an easy choice at the time. I never thought twice about anything that would hold me back along the way.

"Go big or go home," right?

YOU CAN DO ANYTHING YOU PUT YOUR MIND TO... UNLESS IT'S A 'MAN'S' JOB

It was the summer before senior year. I had been volunteering at a local hospital. Part of the hiring process required me to get a tuberculosis test at the employee health center. When the nurse, a friendly woman not more than twice my age, came in, she quickly struck up a conversation and asked me where I was volunteering and what my responsibilities would be. I replied that I was shadowing different departments to see which was the right place for me and told her about my plan to become a doctor.

My excited rambling was met with a response that I will never forget. She said matter-of-factly, "Marry a doctor, be a nurse."

I remember laughing it off at the time and thinking nothing more of it consciously for years. I knew she hadn't meant anything hurtful by it, and I am sure it was similar to the advice that she had gotten when she was attending college. But that was a different time, right? Twenty years ago, women were more likely to be stay-at-home moms raising children and men the successful doctors. But now there are women in science everywhere, aren't there? Working the same jobs as men? Making the same scientific breakthroughs as men? Taking the same journey through college and graduate school as men?

Looking back now, I realize that was the exact moment I should have started thinking about what it would take to live out my dream. It was so clear that her split-second categorization of my gender from her own past experiences led her to believe that I would be more suited to working *under* the doctor than *being* the doctor. Neither she nor I knew at that point that this single, quick conversation would shape my life, or that I would be reflecting on it throughout my college career, and even to this day.

I didn't dig this conversation out of the cobwebs of my brain (beyond laughing about it to my parents later that night) until speaking with my guidance counselor and other teachers about college choices. To my surprise, I was told things such as, "Well, you can always go part-time," and that maybe a Physician's Assistant program would be "a little more suitable for starting a family." I began to think I was being selfish for pursuing this dream and started to investigate other programs. Nursing or midwifery didn't seem that bad. Perhaps I'd even try for a Master's degree in Public Health, something that had flexibility and lacked that "man's job" stigma. What I had contracted was a double whammy of other people's implicit biases and my own self-handicapping, and that was a hard hit to shake off.

THE SIGNIFICANCE OF
SELF-HANDICAPPING

Self-handicapping refers to the way stereotypes ingrained in the unconscious mind can have serious consequences regarding how you see yourself and others and how you choose to behave.[44] The summer before I graduated college, I read Sheryl Sandberg's well-known book *Lean In*,[45] which discusses this widespread phenomenon among women. In one passage, she mentions that a young woman had come into her office and was worried about taking a job because she didn't want to get involved in something that would keep her from having children. Sandberg responded that she should not limit herself for people who do not exist yet and should make the decision that is right for her once they do exist. This has stuck with me as inspiration to not allow others to discourage me.

College is a place for discovering your intellectual talent and increasing your knowledge in subjects that you would like to learn about and understand. It has been described as a place for finding yourself and discovering new opportunities. For some, it's a hub of innovation and success. But this does not mean that colleges exist outside of the realities of gender discrimination and other oppression that many students face. Sometimes unknowingly, the educational system can cultivate an environment where individuals feel as if they are not good enough to be there, thus keeping the already disadvantaged in a cycle that could result in their dropping out.

A student can be powerfully affected by self-handicapping when faced with their peers' and professors' preconceived notions about their academic capabilities. For example, when women are told before the test that there is a gender gap in math test scores before they take a math test, they are more likely to perform poorly. Researchers think this is due to the unconscious stereotype that women are worse at math than their male counterparts. Similar results are seen when African Americans are told their "ability" will be assessed on a standardized test performance, especially affecting women of color. This form of self-handicapping is called stereotype threat.[46]

Stereotypes have been found to be less of a semantic response than they are based on one's own feelings and opinions, as was likely the case when the nurse told me to "Marry a doctor [and] be a nurse." Psychological research, and even brain scan technologies, have helped to elucidate the mechanisms behind this phenomenon, showing the increased stress and self-conscious anxiety that divert cognitive resources from the task at hand.[47] Unfortunately, the way people unconsciously categorize marginalized groups, including women and particularly women of color, continues to cause issues in the world of academia. The #MeToo movement that followed the Sandburg book, mentioned earlier, has powerfully raised that issue.

If self-handicapping is like a confidence problem, in my senior year, I was specifically trying to develop confidence. It is clear to me that when people believe you will perform well, it has a highly positive impact on them and on you. I know it's said that confidence should come from within, but there were many times when I felt like an afterthought to my teachers. For most of my high school freshman and sophomore years, I was quiet, and I tried my best not to get called on in the classroom, which may seem strange as I was always the older-sister-achiever at home. It was not until junior year when teachers started to realize my potential that I started to push myself to participate more. By my senior year, I was much more active in class and finally felt as if I fit in.

Although I felt that I was gaining confidence, I do not recall actually being proud of myself. It didn't help that I had no idea what university I would be attending the upcoming year. After my mom pleaded with me to apply to at least one local school, I decided on the University at Albany. When a letter arrived asking me to apply to the honors college, I was stunned. After a lot more pleading, my mother got me to consider it. I sent in my essay, hardly thinking I had a chance. I stalled opening my acceptance letter for as long as possible, but when I did, I was ecstatic. What that single piece of paper told me was that I, Rachel, a woman, could succeed at college.

Take that, self-handicapping…at least in terms of going to college.

In college, I had other experiences that encouraged me to believe in myself and not follow the path that was recommended. I worked in social science and biological research with professors throughout my undergraduate career and kept my GPA high. I completed all of the requirements for medical school, but when application time came, I did not apply. That 'go big or go home' attitude never stopped driving me to help as many people as possible, and so, I currently find myself working in the medical record industry and attending a graduate program in healthcare administration. By doing this, I hope to operate more on the 'save the world' level rather than the 'save the patient' level. But it is still the same dream to me of having a big impact on people. What is funny looking back on all the times in college I thought about self-handicapping, it was in response to external opinions when what ultimately matters is what was and is my choice. At the time I chose to be pre-med and to pursue what I thought would be a long career in medicine. However, my own ideas of where I wanted to help changed as I came closer to graduating. My concept of how I could help the healthcare industry shifted. And ultimately, I am grateful for my choice.

BACK TO PRE-MED AND THE BASIS OF GENDER SELF-HANDICAPPING

Although women have made good strides toward parity in medical school, having in 2017 achieved more than half of admissions (50.7%) to medical school for the first time,[48] it was not always so. In the 1970s, the figure was under 10%. This gives rise to dated beliefs like the kind Rachel encountered in her story, that some women are simply not cut out for medical education or the life of a doctor. This stands for other professions as well. Recent changes in our culture, including but not limited to the #MeToo or #breakingtheglass ceiling movements, have reinforced the upward trajectory of accomplishment by women and may have also helped weaken the impact of historical discrimination and self-handicapping in the unconscious mind.

It's amazing the progress we have made. Only a few centuries ago, blatantly sexist attitudes were spoken aloud even by influential people, such as the religious reformer Martin Luther (1483-1546), who was quoted as saying, "Girls begin to talk and to stand on their feet sooner than boys because weeds always grow up more quickly than good crops."[49] As authors of this book, we recognize that gender differences continue to exist today. For example, consider the following experiment from 2001.[50] A group of participants were divided into four groups with an equal number of males and females in each group. Each group was to review the performance of a fictional vice president of a large company given the exact same resumes, but it was revealed to one group that the vice president was male and to the other group that the vice president was female. In the review of the male vice president, terms such as 'likable' and 'very competent' were reported, but in the review of the female with the exact same performance record, that 'very competent' dropped to a 'not very competent' rating, although she was still viewed as likable. A third and fourth group were given the same details, but instead, the vice president was a superstar in the field and on a fast track through the company driven by their stellar performance. While the review for the male candidate stayed the same, the female was reviewed as 'not likable' and even 'hostile.'

Clearly, gender biases continue to cause real-world damage. In 2016, a woman named Erin McKelvey had applied for numerous jobs in the STEM industry without receiving a response. A friend by the name of "Alexandra," who had shortened her name to "Alex" for the sake of applications, said she had come across the same thing before shortening her name, and suggested Erin change her name to Mack (her nickname) on her resume. Over the next few months, Erin's callback percentage jumped from 0% to 70%.[51] Though this personal account may seem anecdotal, studies have been done to replicate this observation.[52]

A Yale study surveying over one hundred science faculty from research-intensive universities were asked to rate a student application for a laboratory position. The only difference on the applications was a gender-identifying name. You probably know by now where this is leading: Not only was the fictitious male applicant rated more competent and hirable, they were offered a higher starting salary and more career mentoring. Interestingly, the gender of the faculty member that was hiring did not have any impact on their review, suggesting that this gender bias lives in the subconscious of all people.[53]

SELF-HANDICAPPING, STEREOTYPE THREAT, AND SOME THOUGHTS ABOUT WHAT HIGHER EDUCATION CAN DO ABOUT IT

A very similar concept of stereotype threat was defined by Claude Steele in a 1995 paper as the 'risk of confirming, as self-characteristic, a negative stereotype about one's group.' [54] Stereotype threat explains the many students who avoid putting themselves in challenging situations, such as STEM majors in college, precisely because of the fear that they will fail and become another one of those 'women cannot succeed in this field' statistics. While this chapter takes a gender-based approach to self-handicapping, Steele's original paper focused more on the minority culture (e.g. black) students in taking high-stakes tests like the SAT for determining college admissions. This study not only validated stereotype threat as an explanation for the underperformance of minority participants in standardized tests, but it showed that culture-free tests could not be easily developed as the test-takers added back some of the effects of culture by the way their unconscious brains approached the test. Clearly, culture interacts unconsciously with seemingly objective materials. People who receive lower SAT scores can bring that self-doubt to their college years. This is why encouragement and support, ranging from diversity requirements in general education to education on stereotype threat itself, must be put in motion by educational institutions.

What other forms can institutional encouragement take? There are two forms that we would like to discuss here. The first option is group support by peers in the same situation, who are themselves working to overcome stereotype threat. For someone like Rachel, it could be a women's group of premed female students, especially women from the same ethnic/racial/socio-economic background.[55] Given time, these groups could bond authentically and powerfully inspire each other from their own successes. In the previous chapter, we mentioned a prominent program like this at the University at Albany called the Educational Opportunity Program (EOP), which yields very high retention and graduation rates among groups of students that face barriers to success in higher education. We will return to EOP in the next chapter.

The second option is direct experience in a real-world situation in the workforce, offering applied learning that the controlled atmosphere of the classroom does not offer. For example, an internship in direct patient interaction in a hospital could teach someone like Rachel that she can actually engage in appropriate medical techniques on real patients and do a good job. The same result could be obtained from undergraduate research.[56] Premed students could gain experience in a biomedical laboratory where they manage machines and engage with the concepts of scientific inquiry that underlie the tests and diagnoses of medical patients. Learning by doing creates in the student an unconscious confidence that replaces unconscious self-handicapping. Any source of confidence is good, like developing leadership skills in a summer orientation program. Results may be best though when the experience is in the direct area of self-handicapping, especially if it is blocking a career pathway of interest.

Finally, real individual mentoring is essential to know what groups to place students into or what experiences to nudge them toward. Mentors must truly know a student to be able to help them find the right path, and be both authentic and credible enough with the student to get them to try it. While mentors come in all forms, the one thing they have in common is that they have earned the mentee's trust.

CHAPTER 4

CHRISEL'S STORY:
LOW SOCIOECONOMIC STATUS AND PEER SUPPORT

Defying Gravity

PART I: MAMI

"A few of the motivating factors that bring Hispanic immigrants to the United States include a lack of resources and opportunities in their home countries, abuses of their government, extreme poverty, and even the search for adventure. Each individual might have different circumstances leading to his/her immigration to the United States, but most immigrants have the same general purpose—to make better lives for themselves and their families." [57]

Like every one of our stories, mine begins with a fierce woman of virtue: my mother, also known as Teresa LaPaix. Mami was a strong, independent, Dominican woman, born and raised in Santo

Domingo, a small city that could no longer support the vastness of her vision. The colonization and corruption that riddled her native land made the ideals of America seem worth aiming for. Though she understood that life in America took lots of hard work and no play through the channels of chain migration, she was granted her golden ticket. My mother arrived in New York City at the tender age of 29 and landed on the doorstep of The Red Hook Housing Projects of Brooklyn. She describes the atrocious conditions of the tenement, having to avoid the staircases where shady transactions went down and the dirty elevator walls lined with spit and sometimes even urine. In her advancement, she moved to Tremont Avenue in the Bronx, and later settled in Harlem, where her legacy would slowly, but surely, unfold. Shortly after, my father received his visa, and between the years of 1992 and 1995, she gave birth to three beautiful daughters, and later in 2000, an unexpected son. And even though life became more complex after becoming a mother, factoring in her need to navigate the broken systems of government assistance, she chose perseverance. She knew inherently that her blooming legacy was the highest priority and that she would make it a reality by any means necessary.

FATHERHOOD

"Children who grow up with only one of their biological parents (nearly always the mother) are disadvantaged across a broad array of outcomes... They are twice as likely to drop out of high school, 2.5 times as likely to become teen mothers, and 1.4 times as likely to be idle -- out of school and out of work -- as children who grow up with

both parents. Children in one-parent families also have lower grade
point averages, lower college aspirations, and poorer attendance
records. As adults, they have higher rates of divorce. These patterns
persist even after adjusting for differences in race, parents' education,
number of siblings, and residential location." [58]

My father arrived in New York City in 1992. Already a father
of 5, he set out to America, like many others, in search of better
opportunities. He was the youngest of 12, a political powerhouse
with a balanced set of work skills that allowed him to hustle and
provide for his growing family. A vibrant man with an active social
life, his outings slowly began to take precedence over us, leaving
my mother to do what she could to make sure we were adequately
cared for.

Eventually, she kicked him out of the house in an effort to stand
her ground; however, raising four kids on her own while trying
to manage a blossoming career became difficult and forced her to
bring him back. In 2003, my father suffered a tragic factory accident
that left him temporarily unemployed and disabled.

With financial obligations and a family to support, my mother
stepped up as the main breadwinner and my father became the
caretaker. He would spend his mornings preparing us for school,
his afternoons picking us up, and his evenings looking for work.
On the weekends, he would also take care of us while my mother
took college courses at Bronx Community College with hopes of
attaining a degree, and thus, more money.

His inability to holistically parent created chaotic consequences
for our childhoods. His dictatorial manner left us to experience

harsh forms of discipline under his supervision; he was physically, verbally, and emotionally abusive and not just to us. On top of that, his social life made it all the more difficult for us to co-exist as 'a family.' On one New Year's in particular, his blatant prioritization of his bodega boys over his children was the straw that broke the camel's back. My mother decided that living at the mercy of my father's lifestyle choices was far worse than doing it alone. It was officially over. Our lives changed, yet again.

PART II: LOW SES – HARLEM, NYC

I was born with severe asthma.

"*National surveys indicate asthma risk is particularly high among children with disadvantages in both racial status and socioeconomic status… Reviews indicate low-income children are more likely to consume polluted air and water, live in lower quality housing, reside in more dangerous neighborhoods, and have poorer quality childcare and educational opportunities.*" [59]

As an infant, a near-fatal asthma attack led to my brief demise, but Mami says that she cried out so loud that it reached the heavens and brought me back to life. This moment, among other incidents linked to my asthma, meant I was more coddled as a child than my siblings. With an incessant fear that I would run fast enough to trigger another attack, my mother restricted my playtime, which in a way, stunted my growth. As a child, I was seen as weak. My alpha status did not activate until later on in life and, because of that, I was constantly subjected to bullying, even within the household.

I was the middle child of three sisters, but my scrawny composure could have you thinking otherwise. "La Sufrida" (she who suffers), an aunt labeled me early on. I was Bubbles from the Powerpuff Girls and Michelle from Destiny's Child, so you can only imagine what life was like for me.

Nevertheless, I had my sisters. We were best friends, each other's forever allies and companions, moving through the woes of our circumstances together. In 2000, my mother miraculously gave birth to my brother and the rest is history. We were raised Dominican in the mecca of Black culture, creating space for our multifaceted identities to flourish despite my mother's attempts to keep us in a bubble of Bachata and hair relaxers.

Single motherhood seemed to suit my mother. On the outside, she appeared to have it all together: taking college classes, three kids in private school, bills paid on time. Not all that glitters is gold, though. In our early years, we relied heavily on government assistance, receiving Section 8, WIC vouchers, and Medicaid, which allowed Mami to pay the rent and ensure that we were fed and seemingly healthy. The cost of 'free lunch,' though, was the toxicity that government agencies subjected their participants to. Long lines, nasty verbal treatment, humiliation, and red tape made it all the more of a challenge for my monolingual mother to ensure our needs were met. Still, she thrived. Shit, we all did.

We were held together by the intimate communities within the broader 'hood surrounding us. There were the caretakers who watched over us as Mami made her way home, the local bodegueros[60] who let her slide when the vouchers expired, the old faces from the block who kept her grounded whenever she needed a good word, and the vecina/os[61] who stopped by to share the communal tea with her. They say it takes a village; for us, it took several villages to build up our family. From the block village to the school village to our extended family, we were fortified by the people around us who helped us grow. Through it all, home was where the heart was and that was Harlem, New York. Where we were safe yet in a state of constant hypervigilance, where our Dominican identity was deeply cultivated and our Blackness was fully realized, where we became and bloomed, where our legacies were actualized.

CHILD OF PROMISE: OCTOBER 9TH, 2000 – PERIOD 1 REPORT CARD:

"Chrisel es una niña bilinguie. Ella debe practicar el abecedario – Chrisel necesita terminar su trabajo a tiempo." (Chrisel is a bilingual girl, she should practice her alphabet – Chrisel needs to finish her work on time).

These words marked the beginning of my academic trajectory. As a Spanish-speaking, monolingual 6-year old entering Kindergarten, I was quite clueless to the structures of this new classroom space, and the transition into the ESL program seemed to provide no formal manual. As can be expected from an emotionally overwhelmed child, I struggled to keep up and my weekly spelling tests were a testament to that. When progress report time came around, my teacher had no issue stating the facts.

During our tests, the teacher would reassign seating to everyone except for me. I instinctively realized that she wasn't moving the students away from me for my sake, but more for theirs. After yet another failed spelling test, I went home and approached my mother with the big fat debilitating zero that marked the top of my test paper. She lay on the couch, positioned sideways, her hand on her head, looking downward towards her pregnant belly. I realized she could barely muster up the strength to look up at me and when she finally did, the pain-stricken look in her eyes told me all I needed to know: it was up to me and me alone to do better.

CHILD OF PROMISE: DECEMBER 12TH, 2000 – PERIOD 2 REPORT CARD:

"Gracias a ustedes Chrisel se sabe el abecedario. Ella también sabe los sonidos, los colores, y las figuras geométricas. Muchas Gracias!" Thanks to you Chrisel knows her alphabet. She also knows her sounds, colors and geometric shapes. Thank you so much!

You know how every parent has a favorite childhood story for each child that they'll never forget? This one happens to be my mother's. In a matter of a few months, my spelling test scores went from 0 to 100, literally. While my teacher generously thanked my parents for their help, she had no idea that the mastermind behind this stellar act was, in fact, me. At 6 years old I managed this act of resiliency and independence alone. With a mother that barely spoke the language, weakened by a difficult pregnancy and social-emotional stress, and an absentee father, I had to fend for myself. I'm not sure how or what I did, but it will always remain a testimony to my perseverance, a characteristic that has served me to this very day.

PRIVATE SCHOOL

In the second grade, I graduated from P.S. 36 and entered Corpus Christi, a Catholic school in Harlem. My mother's experience working within the public school system provided her with ample evidence to make certain that her children would not fall prey to the inadequacies of public education. She sacrificed everything in order for us to be adequately educated, often forgoing luxury in order to pay tuition. Mami used to have a two-word jingle she taught us: "Nooo money!" She'd make us repeat it whenever we'd go out, to ensure we'd keep our cravings in check. I later integrated this poverty mentality, learning to get by with the bare essentials. And as our peers flashed their new gadgets while we were getting called down to the secretary's office due to late payments, we grew accustomed to hand-me-downs and whatever Mom could afford.

In my middle school years, my friend's father would call me "Risita," meaning she who laughs. While my living situation merited otherwise, I was indeed full of laughter. I escaped my tumultuous living situation by over-socializing and prioritizing popularity and friendships. In the eighth grade, I took Saturday classes at Notre Dame High School. Notre Dame maintained a close-knit structure and sisterly culture that drew me in. Despite the $7,000 yearly tuition, I knew it was the school for me. It allowed me to strengthen my faith and provided a rigorous college-preparatory curriculum, marking an early opportunity for my inner self to bloom.

Towards the end of my freshman year, I was failing biology, math, and French, and was on the verge of getting expelled.

However, my child-of-promise attitude did not let me slip and time again, I persevered. My junior year, I joined the Double Discovery Program at Columbia University to help me with S.A.T. and college preparation, while also giving me space from my home life. Within this program, I was surrounded by college advisors who supported me in the planning of my future. My eldest sister had been the first in the family to go away to college. In the absence of proper guidance from her school and a lack of knowledge from her family regarding the college process, she wasn't informed of the options for financial assistance available to students like us. Determined to ensure that we wouldn't endure her challenges, she became informed about the Educational Opportunity Program and paid it forward to us. Upon meeting the academic, financial, and S.A.T. score requirements, I was successfully admitted into the program, bringing light into my life beyond the ghetto walls surrounding me.

PART III

"Students within low socioeconomic households tend to attain a lower level of academic skills. This is due to numerous factors of their lifestyles, which in turn affects their academic proficiencies. Poverty, stress, health issues, unsafe neighborhoods, lack of role models and under-resourced schools are a few of the many factors that affect the trajectory of a child within a low socioeconomic household. Many at-risk students, who commonly are minorities, deal with challenges, which can begin during infancy." [62]

EDUCATIONAL OPPORTUNITY PROGRAM

The following is an excerpt from an interview that led to an article in *Diverse Issues in Higher Education* magazine.[63]

"Interviewer: You said your E.O.P. experience got you where you are today. Please explain precisely how?

Chrisel: It was more than financial assistance, it was about access, preparation, and guidance through an experience I'm not sure I would've been able to endure on my own. From the start of my time at the University at Albany, EOP provided me with a family, discipline, and consistent support. I majored in Economics with a minor in Business Administration and became involved in a number of organizations to back to, advocate for, and serve my college community – all of which was facilitated by my network and reach within EOP."

Quietly tucked under the University's Main Library lies a space of family and growth. The University at Albany's Educational Opportunity Program (EOP) provides a safe haven for inner-city youth looking to live out their dreams of prosperity, expansion, and education.[64] This program granted me a formal opportunity to excel, a home away from home, and a redefining of family. Beginning in the summer months before freshman year, I, as an EOP participant, was mandated to attend a pre-college training that provided me the structure and discipline needed to get accustomed to the college environment. University at Albany was unknown territory for me, with no preconceived notions of what college would provide, no Mami and Papi to assist, no formal training of what to expect. EOP housed us and embedded within us the tools we would need for our empowerment. Its seemingly strict measures mirrored many of our upbringings, re-emphasizing the importance of structure through a new lens. We were provided with a preliminary look at how to best shape our upcoming years, given three square meals when most of us were accustomed to less, and offered lectures and classes when most of us had skipped what we didn't care for back in high school. EOP opened us up to a network of support when most of our role models had been 'hood villains.' It provided us with a network of like-minded, equally driven youngsters looking to make it out of the circumstances that had been holding us back.

The bright mornings, birds chirping, trees blowing, and overall quietness of upstate frightened many like myself who were accustomed to the roar of urban jungles. Some didn't make it to the end of the summer program because they couldn't live up to what it required of us, but others persevered mostly because it was our only way out (of poverty) — with nothing else to turn to, we looked to each other for motivation and guidance. In the end, it was everything we needed.

A dynamic leader and fierce advocate, Maritza Martinez, was the face of the program, and alongside her energized staff, she provided all EOP students with every tool needed to find their greatness. After five weeks, my mind and spirit had shifted, and after four years, my life purpose had been found, defined, and refined. To this day, I can undoubtedly thank the EOP program for saving me and many others like me. At the end of my summer experience, I immediately sought to involve myself in advocacy work, the same advocacy EOP provided to me. My trajectory aligned me with a family, a *strong* **dynamic** EOP family bound by our struggle, our potential and our determination to rise by any means. I entered freshman year with this family of over 100 students. We dominated the campus and still dominate the university, as the program has a stronger second-year student retention than the university itself. EOP not only allowed for us to be ourselves, it supported us in discovering our authenticity and provided us with brothers, sisters, aunts, uncles, and a fairy godmother who lifted us up in the process. I am eternally indebted to it.

THE POWER OF GROUPS

The above story emphasizes the power of the group. The use of the word 'family' makes that power clear. This is not the first time that we have encountered the group as a powerful force. In the first chapter, the group is analyzed as a driver of our evolution as a species, leaving with us biological and cultural mechanisms that affect us in more ways than we consciously know. We will return to the group as a force for change in later chapters to discuss more of the social psychological and neuroscientific explanations for this power. We will also take time to consider how higher education might better leverage the group, connecting the 'I' to the 'we', for the growth and development of the individual.

DEFYING GRAVITY

My experiences have allowed me to defy gravity, to triumph over the odds set against me, and to use my story as a shield from the cruel realities of our world all the while empowering others to share their truths and advocate for their lives. Education is considered the first step for human flourishing; it plays a vital role in the development of human capital and is linked with an individual's well-being and their opportunities for better living. Social and economic inequality exacerbates educational inequality and limits the achievements possible for disadvantaged populations, leading to stereotypes, criminality, and further racial, gender, and class division.

I spent four years at the University at Albany, challenging my assumptions of what it meant to be college-educated, while also learning how my upbringing impacted the way I walked in this world. I conducted extensive research on the effects of growing up in a low socio-economic environment on a child's life. I learned about and understood first-hand the constant perpetuation of cycles of poverty and oppression. This research has given me vast perspectives I hope to share with those reading these words. I left college with a sense of security that whatever I would do and whoever I was determined to become, I would never forget where I came from.

Understanding that institutional frameworks were not designed with 'non-traditional' students like myself in mind, I focused on the broader educational aspects available in college. I strengthened my public speaking abilities, fortified my network, developed long-lasting relationships, and chiseled my inquiry-building skills, skills I presently utilize after graduation in community empowerment work through a fellowship at the Coro New York Leadership Center.[65] The symphony of my experiences has ultimately prepared me to live in my authenticity and in the truth of my power. Education was the key to unlock the doors to my limitlessness.

> Where I come from teenage motherhood is the new normal,
>
> Young boys fall susceptible to the pressures of gang life,
>
> And incarceration rates are higher than our local test scores
>
> And in spite of it all, I was able to defy all of what was created to bring me down.
>
> Education is pivotal and everyone deserves equal access and the opportunity to attain one.
>
> "Did you hear about the rose that grew
>
> from a crack in the concrete?
>
> Proving nature's law is wrong, it
>
> learned to walk without having feet.
>
> Funny it seems, but by keeping its dreams;
>
> it learned to breathe fresh air.
>
> Long live the rose that grew from concrete
>
> when no one else ever cared."

Tupac Shakur[66]

CALL TO ACTION:

We must educate families on healthy rearing practices for their children, including reading together and practicing proper communication skills.

We *must* sponsor community-based programming to keep youth active during and after school, engaging them with activities that build leadership and language skills.

We *must* bridge connections between families, communities, community-based organizations and schools in order to assist and advocate for youth in all facets of their lives.

We *must* provide proper funding for school systems in impoverished neighborhoods.

We *must* advocate for more state-funded programs like the EOP, which provides opportunities for students of low socio-economic backgrounds to attend and graduate college.

We *must* provide positive, motivational figures in the lives of at-risk youth, in order to build self-esteem and empowerment.

We *must* create safe spaces for healing from generational traumas to take place.

We *must* make it a priority to allow youth to be who they need to be in order for them to evaluate who they truly want to become.

We *must* LOVE AS IF THE FUTURE DEPENDED ON IT.

CHAPTER 5

MARC'S STORY:

IN-GROUP/OUT-GROUP

Find your niche

AN OPENING WORD ABOUT GROUPS

One of the most powerful themes in this book is the power of the group, which is why we introduced the topic in "Words Matter." Groups and group identification underlie the issues of implicit bias (Chapter 2) and peer support (Chapter 4), for example. So, where does group identification come from?

Social psychologists have long studied the way that we characterize ourselves and those with whom we choose to associate. These natural groups that we often unknowingly form can be based on broad-spectrum similarities, such as religion, culture, or age, or be formed within a much smaller setting like a sports team or college campus. The groups with which you identify yourself are referred to as your "in-groups," while those with which you do not identify are referred to as "out-groups." But here's the catch: You don't just fall easily into a group; rather, you need some common interest or goal that serves to unite you as a team. By having this bond, it gives you a natural "us-versus-them" feeling and can bring even the most seemingly incohesive group of people together, as Marc's story illustrates.

MARC'S STORY

I come from a Jewish household in Williamsville, New York—a small suburb of Buffalo. I was the second of two sons and that, of course, meant I was destined to follow in my brother's footsteps, both figuratively and literally. When I was a kid, this meant copying his actions and his style and constantly fighting with him over his belongings.

When I was finally at preschool age, again I followed in my older brother's footsteps and attended a local school called Child Time. It was here that I developed my reputation as a ham for attention. In this program, once a month, a rotating group of kids would visit local nursing homes to serenade the residents with our singing and percussion skills. I wouldn't say that I was the lead in the choir, but I really enjoyed music and can remember belting out those lines louder than any other child there. I remember how the residents would light up and how I could feel the positive difference we were making in their lives, so I begged every month to join that group of children going to the nursing home. Soon, I got to be the permanent exception to the rotation: I was the first one on the bus every month.

Let's fast forward past the elementary school years of learning how to make friends and the middle school years of learning how to keep friends to July of 2008, the summer before my first day of high school. I received a letter in the mail informing me that, because of where my parents' house was located, I was districted to a different high school than all of my friends that I had worked so long to make and keep. While they would be attending Williamsville North, I would be shipped across the world (about 3 miles) to Williamsville East. Not knowing what else to do, I begged my parents for help. We requested a slot at the next school board meeting, where I pleaded my case, asking them to make an exception for me.

A couple of weeks later, a letter came from the superintendent, which read something like: *Dear Marc, thank you for coming to speak before the School Board. You've been an asset to the Williamsville School District, and we look forward to four more years. Unfortunately, we cannot make an exception, but we appreciate your using the public forum to voice your objection to the closed enrollment. Best of luck in the future.*

Mission failed.

A SMALL FISH IN A BIG POND

It was the first day of school and for the first time ever, I was alone. The bell rang and it was time for that dreaded period: that period with no teachers, that period where everyone would be excitedly telling their friends the highlights of their summer, that period where I would be potentially choosing my fate for the rest of the entire year and knew no one. There seemed to be no friendly faces around, tables were full, and no one was jumping up to ask me to sit with them. It was settled; this was my fate: a small fish in that big pond of the cafeteria, drowning.

A few days passed and reality started to sink in. I began to believe I would be alone forever that my social (im)mobility was etched in stone. My former friends and friend groups were miles away, and I didn't make any step toward joining a new crowd until the second week of school. To this day I can't tell you why, but one kid who reminded me of many of my old friends (involved in clubs, sports, extracurricular activities, and everything that I thought my high school experience would be) grabbed a chair and asked me to join his table rather than sit in a dark corner. With the help of my new friend—my own big fish to emulate—I was blessed with the opportunity to succeed while enjoying myself. I grew while the pond shrunk smaller and smaller. Nothing could stop me now.

Enter college, stage left.

I had done it once. I had survived that transition from no one to someone. But now, I was traveling from one end of the state to the other, a distance that I thought could only be described using units of astronomy. True, I was excited to start this new chapter of my life, but I was also apprehensive about doing it without a support system within arm's reach. I knew I wanted to pursue Public Administration, and the University at Albany had one of the best programs in the nation. I remembered my time from the nursing home, how much joy it had given not only me, but the residents and staff, too. I knew what I had to do. It was time to take that dive again. But this time I was an even smaller fish—and this time, I was swimming in an ocean.

Adjusting to college was not the same. In high school, it was still my hometown, still my district. In Albany, I was outnumbered by down-staters who looked at Western New Yorkers like we were Martians. I began on my own, flying solo without a foothold or a safety net. The memories of those first few days of freshman year of high school in the cafeteria corner flashed back. What if, this time, I didn't find a big fish to swim with?

FINDING MY IN-GROUP YET AGAIN AND TAKING IT ONE STEP FURTHER

When I entered the University at Albany, I was aware of a close-knit Jewish community on campus. While many campuses have one or two culturally or religiously Jewish organizations, the University at Albany had six. From my high school experience, I had learned that the quickest way to enter an in-group was to find a big fish to give me the tools, experience, and peer introductions necessary to build a strong freshman foundation. Among the plethora of Jewish groups and policy-minded students, I grew more comfortable and more confident. It didn't take long before I found myself at Shabbos House most Friday nights surrounded by a group of people who became some of my closest friends.

Though I was still a small fish myself, I did not fall into the self-handicapping mentioned in Chapter 3 that had limited me in high school, and soon I wanted more than to just *emulate* a mentor. I knew that hard work would allow me to establish myself while making a positive, substantive impact. Flashing back to my days as an enthusiastic singer at Child Time's preschool, I knew that I could do more.

One of my new friends was Nick Butler, an extremely involved big fish on campus who introduced me to student government. I saw this as an opportunity to grow and help others while on my journey. Maybe I would even have the chance to be that person who welcomes a nervous new freshman to their first in-group, but let's not get ahead of ourselves. It was only the first few months of the first semester of freshman year.

I decided to kick off my campaign for a "living area" senator (one who represented a specific dorm on campus). During the campaign, I had to speak with people, campaign, and build relationships. Moreover, I had to do it as a freshman on an upper-class quad. Soon, though, I realized that I had not only found my niche, but also a great group of people that shared nearly all of my interests. The amazing part was that this in-group consisted of a diverse population of students, small fish from small towns like me as well as big fish who were already friends with hundreds of students on campus. Students of color and white students, students of varying cultures and religions, students with every imaginable background—we were all blended together as if there were no barriers between us. Though the ocean of students seemed to stay rich in new faces, I found myself growing both within my newfound group and across the campus. Within a few weeks, I was sitting in the Campus Center waiting to hear the results of the election. I won. Finally, everything seemed to be coming together.

GROWING IN THE POND

Social psychologists Herbert Marsh and John Parker introduced the idea of the big-fish-little-pond effect in the 1980s,[67] and since then, it has become a topic of discussion in thousands of works, including Malcolm Gladwell's *David and Goliath: Underdogs, Misfits, and the Art of Battling Giants*.[68] According to this model, individuals innately compare their own self-concept with that of others in a group, and the giftedness of the group conversely determines the potential success for the individual. For example, the big fish in a small pond analogy represents a gifted student in a less-capable group, while a big fish in a big pond refers to a gifted individual in a very capable group. The former of these two individuals would have a higher self-concept than the latter in this situation. Less-talented students are also subject to this psychological effect: when self-worth depends solely on the reference group, the small fish in a big pond has the lowest self-worth of all.

With the help and support of my new friends on campus, I had the opportunity to expand my involvement in student government. Each office brought with it new experiences and new opportunities to make a difference. A first memorable accomplishment was contributing to a policy that made vending machines accept student meal plans 24/7 (which was a surprisingly big step; after all, the way to anyone's heart is through their stomach). Together with a team of outstanding student leaders, the student voice grew more prominent in the University Senate and within the offices of our campus's most senior administrators. We had successful events, engaged in community service, and partnered with organizations to help build the local capital region. I remember looking back at my first few weeks on campus as the small fish from Williamsville, New York, and appreciating all of the people who helped make the vast ocean that was the University at Albany become manageable. Big fish had given me the opportunities necessary to propel myself into a position where I could make lasting change in a place I grew to love.

When I first joined the group that was writing this book, I was vice president of our student government on campus, about to announce my candidacy for president. I had plenty of friends and supporters, name recognition, and a plan forward for the students and our campus. One step at a time, I ran my campaign for the following few months. One foot in front of the other. And as I thought I was gliding to the finish line, I tripped in front of everyone I knew, fell, and internally cried like a baby.

It was a tough election loss, but it served as yet another transformational moment in my life. It taught me more than any class or textbook ever did. It taught me not to take anything for granted. It taught me humility. And it taught me that success is not measured by your victories, but by how you bounce back from failures. It eventually taught me to bring my agency and motivation together to develop the power of self-invention, or re-invention. Though for the first few weeks after the election I felt like everything that had defined me had been thrown down the drain and shredded by the garbage disposal, there was a silver lining.

After I realized that sulking for the rest of my life was not a sustainable solution, losing motivated me to become more deeply involved with the SUNY Student Assembly, the recognized student government organization that brings together SUNY's 64 campuses and 1.4 million students from across New York State.[69] That same year my good friend, Tom Mastro, was serving as Student Assembly Vice President. He declared his candidacy for president and asked me if I would join his campaign. With no doubt in his ability to lead our system to new heights and with some newfound time on my hands, I graciously accepted.

The stakes were as high as it gets in the world of student government. Tom would need to win a majority of votes from delegates across the state. We would need to convince the queens and kings of each castle (the campus student governments) to support his mission and vision. He was running to lead the students in our nation's largest system of higher education. As if that weren't enough pressure, the SUNY Student Assembly president also serves as the sole student member on the Board of Trustees, an influential body that sets the policies for the entire system.

At the Student Assembly convention that April, Tom won. Following the election, he pulled me aside and asked if I would help him implement the vision he had set forth during the campaign. Position-less for the first time since entering college, I accepted his offer to be chief of staff.

Long story short, we kicked butt. During that year I built lasting relationships with students, academics, elected officials, community leaders, and so many other outstanding people. Tom was graduating that next year and I wanted to ensure the great foundation he built was developed even more. The next year, I was nominated to be president and successfully won two consecutive terms. Who would have known that this small fish once content in a school of 200 in Williamsville, New York would wind up swimming its way to becoming a multi-term president of an organization that represents students and campuses across New York State?

The old adage "everything happens for a reason" was the last thing I wanted to hear after my defeat in the campus student body president election. But over and over it rang true, and still does to this day.

GROUP ALLEGIANCE

Given that one of the most basic concepts in social psychology is that humans are social beings who desire social interaction, individuals naturally come together to form groups. Depending on the setting, status as big fish or little fish, and numerous other factors, group exclusivity varies. Once part of a group, without conscious thought, members begin to emulate the attitudes or actions of other members. Naturally, there will be a formation of ranks within the group, with the stronger or more assertive individuals standing out as leaders. Members are typically aware of this hierarchy respective to their place within it, due to the human drive for "in-group" placement. This leaves others, without relationships with those in the in-group, to either remain socially handicapped in the "out-group," lacking the sought-after interaction with other people, or to move on, seeking acceptance in a new group. In Marc's case, though he formed potential relationships with many other students, including the athletes in his new high school and the Jewish students on campus, his group ultimately wound up being a fantastic group of individuals in the student government.

Studies have shown the in-group/out-group effect to form almost anywhere in social settings with humans. Experiments from Henry Tajfel and colleagues conducted in the 1970 and 1980s specifically investigated how little it took for people to form an in-group, the degree to which these people were swayed by in-group thought, and the extent to which the out-group was excluded.[70] Results on the subjects were as you would expect. The natural tendency to form groups was almost inevitable in any social setting. Even if experimentally assigned to a group through random selection, the members of the group were able to identify with their in-group members and form a positive social identity. When given a task of awarding points to in-group versus out-group members, the subjects generally awarded more to in-group members. When the experimental settings were manipulated and point allocation always resulted in the out-group scoring a higher score, the subjects worked hard to maximize the score of the in-group. This supports the importance of the group, rather than just a promotion of competition between the subjects.

With this understanding of the social formation of groups, we wish to reemphasize the nature of social grouping as an innate and natural process. Identification with and belonging in an in-group is critical for human development and even health.[71] For many college freshmen, this means that those first associations you make on campus are critical. Not only is it important to be part of an in-group, it is also important to share a passion with your group members, so that common interests and mutually beneficial relationships form. When strong in-groups positively boost the feelings of inclusion, security, and success of all their members, community building, student success, and retention rates across college campuses follow.

Oxytocin, as discussed in Chapter 1, has the reputation of being the brain's "love hormone" or "cuddle drug." Elevated levels have been extensively studied in regard to mother–newborn bonding, but also have shown to be a result of other positive social bonding experiences, such as looking at a friendly dog.[72] In social settings, oxytocin can increase positive attitudes toward individuals with similar characteristics.[73] These associations can cause the further formation of in-group and out-group membership, even at certain costs. For example, direct administration of oxytocin actually increases the tendency of group members to lie for the greater benefit of the group, as revealed by a 2014 study.[74] This tendency to put the group benefit above that of individual honesty may rely on oxytocin. In another study, participants that had received oxytocin tended to react more strongly to facial expressions of in-group members than those of the out-group wearing the same expression.[75] This result suggests that oxytocin may be critical for our ability to empathize with in-group over out-group members.

Just think of the potential implications this has in regard to our treatment of others even if we do not consciously see them as out-group members (i.e., other sexes, races, ages). With our unknowing willingness to lie for our in-group and our lack of empathy for the out-group, it is easy to see how exclusion, lack of understanding, or even racist tendencies develop. Oxytocin and the brain mechanisms of social cohesion do not help and may produce the out-group problem in the first place. Just think how much this phenomenon complicates the situation for a freshman in college!

BACK TO MARC'S PERSPECTIVE

Throughout my college career, I worked to find my group of friends and expand my circle. My group belonging opened up a world of opportunities at the University at Albany, within the capital region, around the state, and throughout the country. From the latter part of my undergraduate career to now, I have participated in research relating to the retention of students. What causes students to leave? What causes them to stay? Are there certain elements to a college experience that, if fulfilled, guarantee retention? While investigating these questions, I began to offer my own answers. I tried to pinpoint the factors that led to my comfort at the University at Albany. I was "retained," but why? After further reflection, I found that a combination of friendships, mentors, and involvement led to my love for this campus. I mentioned before that I found my niche in student government, and that's true. I also found my niche in student groups like the Jewish organization, Hillel. Utilizing my time in college to enrich my Jewish heritage was a worthwhile experience and, again, gave me access to that first in-group on campus. Making new friends at Shabbat dinners and during holidays will always serve as a centerpiece of my time in college, and I still often wonder if I would be that kid sitting alone at the dark, dusty table back in high school if it wasn't for my acceptance into this crowd soon after I made it to campus.

For an institution of higher education to reach its full potential, student retention is critical. Ensuring a large and well-educated graduating class to spread their positive experiences about their time in college is beneficial for both the graduate and the institution.

Because of the people who helped me to overcome my feelings of being in the out-group, I had no doubts about completing my 4 years. I bet you can guess where I remained for my master's degree as well.

On campus, I saw that students from minority backgrounds are oftentimes marginalized and, due to a lack of inclusion, struggle with finding their in-group on campus. Studies show that engaging with relatable individuals offers validation and results in a sense of belonging.[76] Our need for validation stresses that students, especially during the early stages of an academic career, need to feel authentic reinforcement from peers and advisors to develop a sense of belonging. This means that not only do students need this in-group feeling, they also need validation to succeed and progress throughout their program, just as we saw in earlier chapters. For me, it wasn't just about finding my in-group, it was about reciprocated acceptance and appreciation. For many, myself included, the transition to college is the most significant change they have faced. I did my best to "pay it forward" by offering all the tips and tricks I could to incoming freshmen at campuses across the country.

SOCIAL NEUROPSYCHOLOGY OF GROUPS

As discussed, we know that the group has a tremendous effect on individual decision-making that goes beyond famous studies of conformity[77] or psychophysiological health.[78] It is built into our brains, perhaps a result of group advantages for individual survival that promote group behavior. That was why it was so important to Marc in high school to have one of the "cool kids" (in-group) seek to socialize with him by grabbing a chair and asking him to "join his table."

In-group/out-group mentality affects all that we do. In politics, we have seen the negative consequences of our group psychology, as tribalism is fomented by social media and direct us-vs.-them leadership. New terms, like "Hivemind," [79] reflect this groupthink. This term was derived from exactly what you would think, nearly two decades of work from a scientist named Thomas Seeley on the study of honeybee swarms and their group problem-solving that leads to the survival of the colony as a whole.[80] Our focus, however, is on how in-groups can be harnessed to create positive results in a diverse college population.

CHAPTER 6

AGATA'S STORY:

STEREOTYPE THREAT

—

The fear of starting over

I was born in a small town in the southeast of Poland. As a child, I traveled back and forth between Poland and the United States. This traveling back and forth became very painful, so my mother and I decided that we wanted to move permanently to New York to live with my father. I was 14 years old. Imagine yourself at that age switching schools, with new friends, new teachers, and all of the other anxieties that come with moving. Now imagine adding a move across the world, to a country with a new language, a city you had only just visited in the past, a new culture, new home, new everything. I did not know what I was in for.

We lived in New York City, specifically in the borough of Queens. When it came time to enroll in a high school, my parents submitted my application to Forest Hills High School, a few miles from the new place I was living. I remember it was a hot summer day when my father received a phone call from the school's administrator regarding my status. I was accepted! But there was a catch: The school required that I take a 5-hour English proficiency exam in order to determine what grade level I would be placed in for my first year in this big new city.

It was the exam of a lifetime. As the day got closer, the fear of the unknown took over. I was panicking. Finally, the day came. My parents took me to the school and I remember trying to catch my breath and look composed, like I had any confidence whatsoever. There I was: sitting face to face with one of the deans. There was no turning back. It was now or never; my fate would be decided with this one dreaded exam with four parts: speaking, listening, reading, and writing. Although I had taken some English classes back in Poland, I didn't feel prepared. All of the words seemed to leave my head when the dean started to ask me questions, a symptom I would later come to associate with the phenomenon of stereotype threat. Luckily, my parents were beside me, and I know that if it wasn't for their support, I would not have been able to complete the exam.

The results came immediately. To my surprise, I was placed in a grade higher than anticipated. Nevertheless, since I was still uncomfortable with the English language, after speaking with my parents, we requested that I be placed in the middle of freshman instead of sophomore year. Immediately when I started, I was placed in the English as a Second Language (ESL) program, which lasted for a year and a half. Although I had tested into a higher grade level, being placed in this rudimentary program frankly made me feel as if I had a learning disability. That was the common view of such programs by other students in the school and members of my society. In later years, I've learned that students in ESL programs are even looked down on by some teachers, who think they bring their overall testing scores down. And it hurt. I felt like an outsider in a new society with a new language, and it made my freshman year a nightmare.

Despite my feelings, I pushed myself to engage in learning everything the ESL program had to teach, as I knew this knowledge would help me grow. Beyond my self-doubt, being part of an immigrant family meant I had a determination to not let them down. It took time, but with the help of my teachers and parents, I gradually started to feel more comfortable with my English and began to appreciate the program more and more. I came to understand at a gut level that this system, far from serving as a punishment to force a negative label on myself and my classmates, was in place to help students like me overcome our language barriers. Month after month, I got better at communicating with my peers. I was making friends and performing very well academically in all of my classes. By the time I reached my senior year of high school, having completed this ESL program and all of my other classes in strong standing, I was placed in two advanced placement classes: psychology and art history. This might seem like a small victory, but it really felt to me as if it were the first step toward a newfound confidence. I could do it; I could succeed in this English-based, American system of learning.

A PSYCHOLOGY CLASS AND A FEW MORE

Psychology class senior year was my favorite part of the day. The minute I sat down at my desk, I felt like a brand-new person: confident, excited to learn, and focused. I really *got* the material being taught. It made me feel like all that struggle in the beginning was worth it. I was stimulated and driven to know more about the field. This was when I decided that psychology was my "thing." I remember always leaving class to find myself in the library researching articles online, ultimately subscribing to *Psychology Today*. I began to read about how humans behave in certain ways, why they feel happy or sad, how they experience pleasure, and how they deal with pain. I was hooked: The brain was a fascinating thing. As I learned more and more, the overarching question that emerged for me was, "What factors trigger our behavior and what mechanisms are involved in learning?" I wanted to know it all, and in order to do that, I decided I needed to go to college.

I signed up to take the SAT without knowing exactly what to expect. Replaying that English proficiency exam in my head from three years earlier, I had a bit of anxiety, but thankfully I performed very well (another small victory, of course, for my self-confidence). I applied to Queens College and immediately declared Psychology as my major. The first semester at Queens went very smoothly; I began taking the courses required toward my major, and my fascination continued to grow.

During my second semester on campus, I stumbled upon a course called Psychology 103: "Pleasure and Pain." I immediately felt drawn toward this course because of all the readings I had done back in high school. The course met twice a week, taught by two neuroscientists and psychology professors, Dr. Stellar and Dr. Bodnar, and discussed the basic neuroscience of pleasure and pain systems. The course also touched on biological, neurochemical, sociological, and evolutionary theories about pleasure and pain systems. I remember being that overly excited student on the first day of class, eager to learn with a smile on my face, and that feeling did not once fade over the semester.

After completing the 103 course, my curiosity and seemingly endless questions led me to the office of Dr. Stellar. We fell into long discussions about Dr. Stellar's experience teaching students who, like me, had some self-doubt when entering Queens College, perhaps due to the difficulties of being an immigrant. Those conversations were, at first, centered on a blog he had just posted with another student called "The Social Brain and the Experiential Education in and out of the Classroom,"[81] exploring how experiential education principles can work inside the classroom. I felt comfortable with Dr. Stellar and became very interested in this research, and particularly in how the flipped-hybrid course structure could bring more active engagement out of students experiencing self-doubt.[82] This was all new territory for me, but the more I read about the research behind this teaching style, the more I could see that the experiential approach was key to getting students involved in their education.

Maybe this form of education can challenge the brain in a new way; maybe this was the key to reaching students like me. There was only one way to find out. Three months later, I dove in headfirst. Dr. Stellar hired me as an undergraduate research assistant to help him develop and then do research on his introductory course using this method in the fall of 2014. That's when we decided to write our own blog on the course that was posted in 2015.[83]

That was the ultimate experience for me as a former ESL student who once seriously doubted herself. It is exceeded only by being involved in the writing of this book.

A WORD ABOUT FLIPPING THE CLASSROOM TO BREAK DOWN WALLS OF SELF-DOUBT

The "Introduction to Psychology" class we developed was scheduled to meet every week on Wednesdays and Fridays in the fall semester of 2014. We decided to cancel the Friday classes, making it a hybrid course. A hybrid course is designed to function by combining face-to-face and online formats. On the day we did not meet, students were instructed to watch YouTube videos made by Dr. Stellar, discussing the main concepts of each chapter. On the in-class day, before the lecture began, students were required to take a short quiz (approximately two questions) about the videos. In addition, as part of the hybrid nature of the course, they read textbook chapters about the week's topics and answered 25-30 multiple choice questions on Learning Management System software on a computer in the comfort of their home. These questions served as additional practice to prepare for upcoming exams and supported the in-class attendance on Wednesdays.

At the end of every lecture, I gave out index cards to students and asked them to write one positive and one negative opinion, anonymously, about the course structure or material. After collecting the cards, we entered the data into an Excel sheet for later analysis. The results were shared with students every week, demonstrating where the course could be improved from their perspective, and based on the results, we worked together each week to modify our in-class activities. The continuous modification of the Wednesday lecture and overall course activity added to the flipped classroom's ability to increase student engagement. I think the fluidity, growth, and student involvement in the development of this course throughout the semester was absolutely essential to its success.

From this experience, I realized that I wanted to continue working with professors to help students like me accomplish their academic goals; more specifically, to help them learn the course material more effectively. That's why I worked with Dr. Bodnar as a discussion leader in the "Pleasure and Pain" course for two consecutive semesters, during which I learned more about his research on conditioned flavor preference in different strains of mice. I even decided to volunteer in his neuroscience lab, in hopes of learning more about how research actually works in a laboratory setting. I had come quite a long way from the self-doubter who first entered the ESL program in high school.

STEREOTYPE THREAT AND WHY IT MATTERS

As mentioned in Chapter 3 on self-handicapping, the term "stereotype threat" was first introduced into social science literature by Claude Steele and Joshua Aronson in 1995.[84] Here we focus more on the essence of belonging to a group (in this case, an immigrant Polish population that did not speak English well) that can lead to underperformance in tasks in which this group is not "supposed" to perform well (excelling in high school). The stereotype threat concept provided an important alternate explanation of persistent gaps between the performance of individuals inside and outside the majority culture on standardized tests, like the SAT.

The results of their 1995 study challenged common group stereotypes. They found that when the same challenging verbal test from the GRE was administered to black and white college students after they were told that the test was a diagnostic of future performance, the black students underperformed the white students. However, when the same exact test was administered under non-diagnostic conditions (e.g., just for fun), the difference disappeared. The study's implications for the interpretation of SAT test score discrepancies between black and white students landed it in the spotlight. While the study has been both criticized and defended, it remains a staple of modern social psychological thinking about groups. The results of the study are not surprising when considered more deeply: If a group an individual belongs to is discriminated against based on a stereotype of academic inferiority, a test that is said to assess ability would raise stress levels and reduce confidence, resulting in poorer performance.

Neuroscience also supports the result of this social psychology study. A brain-scan study in 2008 investigated stereotype threat in women based on underperformance on a math or mental rotation test that is seen as favoring men.[85] In the study, the ventral anterior cingulate cortex was found to be activated under stereotype threat conditions in a way that correlated to the amount of underperformance. This makes sense: The anterior cingulate cortex area is associated with a variety of performance self-monitoring and error-detection functions. This brain area also, alongside other prefrontal cortex areas, regulates emotional reactivity, including fear responses that involve the amygdala.[86]

THE ACADEMIC JOURNEY TO OVERCOMING IMMIGRANT STEREOTYPE THREAT

The education system had once labeled me as an ESL student, which was something others easily made fun of at the time. The reputation of this group as "stupid" found me falling victim to stereotype threat. It undermined my confidence, like the story told in Chapter 3.

Reflecting on my academic journey, I learned that life as an immigrant can be overwhelming and that I had the capacity to underestimate my abilities, particularly my English-language skills, due to harmful stereotypes. My struggles taught me that motivation is key to accomplishing our goals. Ultimately, I thrived in the ESL program and completed it within a year and a half. I established friendships and professional relationships with my mentors and teachers, which boosted my confidence and empowered me to become a more active participant in my own education.

Providing students with constant support, resources, and personalized learning environments enhances effective learning. My direct involvement in the psychology courses and my hands-on experiences in the laboratory while I was at college showed me that student engagement is necessary in the learning process. Overall, I have learned that anything is possible, including overcoming even the most negative stereotype threats, with social support, determination, and trust.

Mutual understanding of motivations and emotions between students and teachers builds trust in the classroom. We are all different from one another; therefore, we are motivated by different things. We choose whether we want to participate in class on a given day, or to simply not care at all. There are few reasons why either choice might happen. It can depend on our own personality, or whether or not we have established a trustworthy relationship with our professor.

In my opinion, there are a few principles that we must consider while considering students' motivation and trust building with professors:

First is the alignment between an individual's goal and the goal of the classroom at large. It is important to harmonize these goals as much as possible. That way all students feel invested and are more willing to work toward the main goal of the class.

Second is the teacher's recognition of students' competencies. It is important that the teacher acknowledges something unique about each one of the students and helps them in the work toward achieving their goals.

Third is providing appropriate and realistic goals for all students. If we expect too much from students, they may get discouraged and be less likely to work with us. We could also lose their trust.

This brings us to the final important element in the classroom. *Motivation*, divided into intrinsic and extrinsic forms, plays a big role in the way students learn and apply their newly learned information. When talking about intrinsic motivation in college, we think of students who possess a fascination for a subject, come equipped with a ready sense of its relevance to their life and the world, and have a desire to master it. These students are usually highly motivated and cooperative and have developed a good student-teacher relationship. Extrinsically motivated college students, on the other hand, have a need to earn some type of reward or meet parental expectations; for example, by getting a good grade on the exam. These students probably won't participate as much in classroom activities or care for a strong student-teacher relationship, tending to do mainly the required work. Obviously, intrinsic motivation is the best for student success, especially if one has to overcome stereotype threat. The question is how we get there.

LESSON: TEACHERS CAN MOTIVATE STUDENTS TO OVERCOME STEREOTYPE THREAT IN THE CLASSROOM

How do teachers reach out to intrinsically motivate students? This is particularly important in overcoming stereotype threat. According to Matt DeLong and Dale Winter,[87] there are a number of strategies. First of all, the teacher should strive to be a role model for the students. It is important that the classroom is being led with enthusiasm and good energy. When the students see that the teacher is passionate about a subject, it will often automatically motivate the student to want to learn about the topic. A second important strategy is for professors to get to know the students, if possible, depending on class size. To do that, teachers must display a strong interest in their students' different learning styles, support their educational goals, and have faith in their abilities. It's a good idea to use lots of examples in order to help the widest range of students understand concepts better, stay engaged, and integrate their learning. Additionally, teachers can show students how the course prepares them for future opportunities so that they do not feel like what they learn will go to waste. If students can see a pathway for their own growth, it is more engaging than purely academic textbook learning.

Another great strategy for engaging students is the use of various student-active teaching activities. These activities directly encourage students to participate, provide positive social pressure from the group, and demonstrate their level of mastery in a way that is not possible when students simply listen to a lecture. It is important to set realistic performance goals and help students achieve them by encouraging them to set goals for themselves based on their own abilities. This involves teachers placing appropriate emphasis on testing and grading, meaning that tests should always reflect the students' realistic ability to apply the learned knowledge. It is also important to balance the praise and constructive criticism you give students. Both can be motivating, but only provide negative comments pertaining to particular performances and not the performer themselves. The teacher has to be sure that they are giving nonjudgmental feedback so that the student does not get discouraged. And last but not least, the teacher should give students as much control over their own education as possible, letting the student learn at their own pace. For example, teachers can give their students a variety of assignments to pick from, including papers and projects, in order to give them control over how they will choose to show their understanding of the material and demonstrate their ability to apply their knowledge outside of the classroom.

As a side note we want to mention here that while stereotype threat is a well-accepted social psychological phenomenon and is used in our book and by others to understand why some students might struggle in a college class because they define themselves as not "book smart" or as handicapped by language skills or even supposed intrinsic ability, there are some reasons to be a bit cautious. We humans have a natural tendency to be less skeptical of data that fit our accepted notions—a phenomenon once called the "file drawer effect,"[88] where studies that cast doubt on a dominant theory are put into a file drawer rather than being published. However, as authors we are convinced by the evidence for stereotype threat.[89]

In this story, Agata certainly felt the effects of stereotype threat, as if the ESL title labeled her as someone who would not succeed in school. Yet she did it. On the other hand, sometimes a label like ESL is helpful, as witnessed in a 2017 study of West Virginia ESL students where graduation rates exceeded those of non-ESL students.[90]

We have and will continue to argue for the power of the Educational Opportunity Program (EOP), demonstrated by their high graduation rates.[91] EOP could be seen as another label that diminishes student self-worth, yet it seems to have the opposite effect.

In the last chapter, we will discuss how we can fight these negative phenomena with a suite of positive unconscious learning opportunities, including mentoring, peer support, and other factors that contribute to the self-perception and motivation of students in and out of the classroom. It is this engagement that results in the intrinsic motivation and confidence that help overcome the natural self-doubt attached to our identities and that apply to us all.

CHAPTER 7

CONCLUSIONS:
EXPERIENTIAL EDUCATION IN LEVERAGING DIVERSITY

———

The following words are geared towards all higher education institutions as we collectivity fortify our efforts in teaching diversity education. To administrators, university educators, and student leaders of diverse and/or majority cultured institutions, we speak directly to you as we all play a role in addressing the need for cultural awareness and competency throughout diversity learning. We are almost entirely a collection of former students who, while applauding and supporting the work in progress, also want to suggest points of improvement based on our own experiences. Our stories are largely based on our undergraduate journeys at both The University at Albany and Queens College of New York. We acknowledge these institutions as incredibly diverse communities with a mission and demographic that mirror the changing colors of our nation. We are indeed privileged to have been able to strengthen our understanding of self and the collective through an education at a culturally diverse institution and note that this may not be the case for every individual reading this book. However, we do hope that whatever discussions open after this book is read, it involves the students as strong partners in figuring out how to move forward.

WHAT DO WE MEAN WHEN WE TALK ABOUT DIVERSITY? AND WHAT ARE WE CONSIDERING DIVERSITY LEARNING TO BE?

Diversity: The practice, mindset, or quality of including or involving people *from a range of different social and ethnic backgrounds and of different genders, sexual orientations, and more.*

The stories you have just read just begin to scratch the surface in addressing racial, socioeconomic/class, gender-based, ethnic, religious, and linguistic diversity. There are so many more forms of diversity, including diversity of age, sexual orientation, gender identity, and able-bodiedness. In most university settings, administrators, professors, and students encounter these forms of diversity. This list is by no means exhaustive. In fact, the word diversity is so broad that the topics it opens for exploration are truly limitless. We see that as a strength of the word, rather than something to shy away from.

In this final chapter, we would like to clearly state that diversity learning through racial, gender, and other awareness and an equity mindset is crucial to the prosperity and harmony of an academic institution. This multi-layered educational journey can begin at any level. In this case, we insist that the task be a primary responsibility of the administrators of colleges and universities. Once the university has acknowledged the importance of this form of learning, educators can help students appreciate differences among their classmates and others in the world through the teachings of different cultures and histories.

Within the last decade, educational institutions all over the country have made drastic advancements in their inclusivity efforts and that has greatly accelerated with the black lives matters movement. This level of tenacity is needed for higher educational institutions at all levels to expand their potential. We acknowledge the ways in which progress has been achieved, ranging from expansions of cultural studies departments to general education requirements focused on diversity and inclusion. It is to higher education's further credit that these diversity courses are overwhelmingly taught by faculty members who are passionate about their discipline and who bring that passion to their teaching. Not only do students learn key historical and present-day analyses of social justice topics, but they also often learn how to personally position themselves with regard to these concepts. This practice is often called faculty mentoring, allowing students to question and examine concepts at an individual and personal level. In addition, colleges and universities typically schedule special workshops or teaching programs on key topics, like the ones we have seen mentioned in the story chapters 2 through 6.

AND YET THERE IS STILL MORE
THAT CAN BE DONE.

We see the transformative power of inclusive spaces, where people of all races, ethnicities, passions, and abilities can come together and thrive. We note the potential for direct student experiences across identity groups to expand learning and foster career development for after college. We see this experiential work as brain-natural, meaning that it has a powerful impact on unconscious decision-making processes. These experiences are important in a variety of life circumstances. The impact of the experiential process, which is defined as "learning through experience," or more specifically as "learning through doing with reflection on that doing," can be easily missed, given the standard higher education focus on in-classroom learning. It is all too common for the experiential side of learning to be set aside solely as extra-curricular. We would like to suggest something different can be added to the classic academic curriculum-based efforts.

Today, we are witnessing an evolution in the type of employees that businesses are looking to hire straight out of college. These businesses want students with some work experience and a host of what some call "soft skills" and others call "power skills," like communication, organization, and the ability to work in teams. To support career development, some colleges and universities are committing across the board to early internships or even alternating full-time work and study periods in a cooperative format. Public pressure and student debt have made it important for students to combine academic learning with an experiential focus in order to gauge what they might do when they graduate. Internships are everywhere in higher education, as are other experiential activities like study abroad or research positions.

Now we need the same resources and effort placed into experiential learning intertwined with cross-cultural education. This must be seen as inseparable from the learning process. In the current higher education environment, diversity learning from direct experience is found in extracurricular projects such as community or service-learning, or it is celebrated in the arts, music, or theater productions. To its detriment, diversity learning is often relegated to the Diversity and Student Life Offices. In this arrangement, we are led to believe that diversity learning is on the "side-burner." It will remain there until experiential learning about diversity becomes integrated with the whole university, including the academic side. Only then will it gain the power to really transform a student's mind. Only then will higher education rise to its full teaching potential, as it responds to the needs of our global world.

In order to enhance higher education with these fulfilling learning experiences, we must address the challenges of (A) how to expose majority-culture and all students to people different from them and experiences that differ from their own, and (B) how to make our campuses a safe and inclusive space for non-majority-culture students.

HOW TO EXPOSE ALL STUDENTS TO PEOPLE DIFFERENT FROM THEM AND EXPERIENCES THAT DIFFER FROM THEIR OWN

- **Look for opportunities to explore an out-group yourself.** Reach out to a group you would not necessarily have gravitated to naturally. If you are in a position of leadership, ask how you can team up with them to accomplish a common goal.

- **Lift up your classmates.** This can take a lot of emotional energy. It is not your sole job, of course, to partner with a student. If you can, great. But in lieu of that, find opportunities to raise up your classmates' voices, particularly those that are underrepresented in their career paths and/or marginalized. Be an ally.[92] Speak up when a member of these groups is interrupted. Return focus to the fact that they were sharing an idea. Express interest in what they have said and ask them to continue. Point out opportunities for them.

- **Reach out to students who may have similar interests but are from different groups.** Encourage them to join your (formal or informal) group. It may not happen overnight, but it starts with helping them feel comfortable. The best ambassadors for the ideas in this book are you, students, as peers. The fact is that many students feel uncomfortable talking about these issues. Some campuses provide training and other programs, but there is nothing wrong with a simple conversation as long as it is respectful. If you have a common interest, that is a good start.

HOW TO MAKE OUR CAMPUSES A SAFE AND INCLUSIVE SPACE FOR NON-MAJORITY-CULTURE STUDENTS.

- **Start diversity clubs, organize activities, and create organizations.** All of the hard work to establish groups, attract members, and create engaging activities is worth it when you meet up with a passion for your chosen cause and a desire to bring people together.
- **Communicate with your professors and find diversity mentors.** Professors are already mentors by virtue of subject knowledge, but you could talk to them about other diversity issues on your campus. If that mentoring relationship can cross into subjects outside your area of study, that is even better.
- **Do not let your university off the hook.** Get to know key administrators. Meet with them. Keep a dialogue open. Do not stop respectfully pushing.

First and foremost, we must accept diversity as a foundational value of life. Embracing diversity as a core value is necessary to take full advantage of the sought-after personal and professional benefits found on a university campus, in the workplace, and in the daily interpersonal relationships that make up our lives. This is an integral part of the path of progress for every student towards their graduation and career development. Inclusion and cross-cultural education expand a student's emotional intelligence, improve unconscious decision-making, and reinforce the facts-and-theories knowledge gained academically.

The stories told in chapters 2 through 6 were curated with five diversity-related principles in mind, selected from a large pool of possibilities. To review, we have included implicit bias, self-handicapping, group dynamics/peer support, in-group/out-group, and stereotype threat. In this final chapter, we take a slightly different approach, as we combine these story chapter topics to arrive at two major overarching themes: First, the power of the group, and then the agency of the individual. After that discussion, we will highlight examples of experiential learning intertwined with diversity experiences to develop topics such as student leadership, study abroad, and the value of mentoring. Finally, we will give some recommendations on how to enhance implicit learning through inclusion.

We want to acknowledge, in advance, that there are many experts with powerful scholarship and personal histories in this important field. We have cited a few examples of this great body of scholarly and persuasive work, but it is not our goal to compete with this knowledge, nor to write a proscriptive list of suggestions for what to do. Rather, we want to spark some additional thinking on the topic and encourage a conversation within and among educational institutions about the intersection of diversity and education. While many places are already doing this work and may find some suggestions helpful, others may be inspired to start now.

We also believe that for us all to live in an open and civil society, it is important for its members to understand each other more rather than less and to do so at both a conscious and an unconscious decision-making level. Today's college students should consider finding more ways to build connectivity that extends beyond racial barriers. This will have a ripple effect on post-college job success in industries that compete globally (and they all do) because having both types of academic and direct experience with issues of diversity will help our students get, retain, and be productive in those jobs. As a business chairperson in the World Economic Forum said:

We live in a complex, interconnected world where diversity, shaped by globalization and technological advance, forms the fabric of modern society. Notwithstanding this interconnectedness, there is also growing polarization – both in the physical and digital worlds – fueled by identity politics and the resurgence of nationalist ideals.[93]

Not surprisingly, our workplaces tend to mirror the sociocultural dynamics at play in our lives outside work. Having built and scaled a multinational enterprise over nearly two decades, I have learned that diversity in the workplace is an asset for both businesses and their employees, in its capacity to foster innovation, creativity, and empathy in ways that homogeneous environments seldom do. Yet it takes careful nurturing and conscious orchestration to unleash the true potential of this invaluable asset."

We already see increasing attention to the wide-ranging topics and issues college students care about. The students are starting it on their own, sometimes with demonstrations of support for their own causes. In some cases, they are even leading the higher education institutions they attend. We now call on higher education as an industry to join them and help them with experiential programs targeted at changing the culture.

THE GROUP: IMPLICIT BIAS, GROUP SUPPORT, AND IN-GROUP/ OUT-GROUP DYNAMICS

We start our summary discussion by combining the major themes from Chapters 2 (implicit bias), 4 (group support of the individual), and 5 (in-group/out-group). Our focus here is on social group dynamics. We believe:

- The unconscious decision-making that occurs in a given in-group about an out-group strongly contributes to implicit bias.
- Groups can be a powerful factor in creating individual success.
- Finding a place within a group can be an important factor for student success.

We would like to open with a review and discussion of the Educational Opportunity Program (EOP) program at the University at Albany, which was mentioned in both Beny's and Chrisel's stories (Chapters 2 and 5, respectively), and which powerfully illustrates the above three points.

Since its founding a half-century ago, EOP has been helping students of limited financial means succeed in the college experience. A gateway to educational prosperity, the testimonies of EOP scholars and the stellar trajectory of the program provide us with the evidence to further understand the importance of group bonding, peer to peer support, and motivation. EOP was based on the SEEK (Search for Education, Elevation, and Knowledge) program started at the City University of New York (CUNY) system and is parallel to HEOP (Higher Education Opportunity Program) at independent New York State colleges and universities. Today, EOP is on nearly 50 campuses at SUNY, including the University at Albany. The remarkable results of the University at Albany EOP program lend us most of our inferences, and we believe the program can serve as a useful model for other colleges and universities. There are other colleges, universities, and systems with similar programs, but for our purposes, we will analyze EOP as one model for helping a diverse community of students adjust to the college environment and serving as a catalyst for their own positive campus contributions.

Statistically, at the University at Albany, EOP cohorts out-perform the university as a whole. Over 90% of EOP freshmen become sophomores, exceeding the university's retention rate by about 10%. In terms of the ultimate graduation rate, again EOP students currently outperform the University average, this time by about 6%.

A bonded group that is close like a family has power over us as individuals, influencing our decisions on a conscious and unconscious level. We see that effect in sports teams and in the military, which both use a "boot camp" experience to bond their participants. It is that combination, particularly the influence on unconscious decision-making, that we think is relevant in producing the remarkable levels of student success. The program at the University at Albany employs a very serious and rigorous

5-week summer residence program for prospective freshmen who have been offered undergraduate admission but have not yet started school. In fact, the EOP students must successfully pass the summer program to be fully admitted to the university. While many useful academic skills are taught in EOP, it is the bonding and discipline infused into it that we think makes the biggest difference.

The in-group dynamics at EOP boil down to strong bonding amongst the students themselves and between the students and their advocates. This bond creates what the EOP members often self-describe as a family, and that "family" provides strength and motivation for their individual efforts at college. When an individual student in EOP struggles, it is the EOP family that backs them up and provides the social support and resources needed to help them succeed. This group-individual bonding dynamic is what we want colleges and universities to create. Bonding in EOP may come from the relative isolation of being on campus over the summer or the collective struggle of the experience. EOP's success is likely enabled by the general coherence of the group. As a largely minority population that typically does not have the financial, social, or academic advantages of majority-culture students, a group coherence is facilitated that amplifies the success of the group by setting a purpose to the struggle that the EOP summer students share.

This introductory period to the college world provides many first-time college students a priority download on the college environment, the social experience, and their individual journey. One sophomore student revealed that even though the university is large (about 18,000 students), when she sees someone on campus who she recognizes from that summer program, it brings back the still-vivid bonding experience that happened, in her case, more than a year before.

A final related factor that applies to any such program is the leadership, including the staff, advisors, and teachers of the summer program, first-year program, and subsequent years of the EOP student's college education. Uniformly, they hold the program as a space of excellence and are eager to pass that viewpoint to the individual students within it as long as, of course, *they earn it.* Thus, the EOP's spirit is a personal and passionate tradition that each previous director carries and passes on to the current director. To us, EOP has the characteristics of a very large family: students sometimes even refer to the director as "mother." In turn, the leadership knows every students' name, story, and circumstances. One student recently told us that he could not fail in school because he could not fail the director of the program, followed by himself and his biological family at home. The power of the group is felt deeply within this program. The strong ties of those within the program, combined with their inner grit, lead to triumphant stories of intrinsic motivation, perseverance, and success.

GROUP-SPANNING ACTIVITIES

What makes EOP even more special is that even in a resource-stretched public-university environment, the program maintains its focus on helping individual students, regardless of whether the student is in the program or not. When Provost Stellar came to the University at Albany in 2015 and noticed the retention power of the EOP, he conducted a survey of a few dozen students whose profiles resembled those of EOP students, even though they were not formal members of the program. The informal survey simply asked them if they would be interested in the program benefits that EOP students receive. From the universal answer, Provost Stellar learned that when students outside of the program sought help from EOP, they always received the support they needed. The EOP is inclusive even beyond its members. Many respondents were from minority communities and shared that one of the reasons they selected the University was due to its diversity, a diversity that is attributed in large part to the EOP program.

WHERE THE UNIVERSITY COMES IN

Colleges and universities can build collective levels of motivation by encouraging their students to identify strongly with the diversity present in their institution. If your university is not racially or ethnically diverse, a good place to start is to identify the types of diversity that certainly *are* present in your student body. This diversity might include gender, sexual orientation, religion, political affiliation, disability, and other life experiences (like having traveled widely or being from a military family). Once you have identified potential ways to bridge existing gaps and bring people together, you can then cultivate engaging student activities, spaces for discussion, and opportunities to attract new groups as the university builds its focus on diversity as a foundation for success. This step, followed by organizing discussions and putting protocols in place, is itself a good start to helping individuals within that institution come together more.

Often, you will find that the approach comes naturally. Ever notice the pride for a big season sports game? Or the excitement over banquets, fashions shows, or cultural conferences? Sporting and cultural events are examples of campus harmony, for example, where tens of thousands of students, alumni, and faculty pack a stadium on the weekend to cheer on the university's team. It is important to produce success of which the entire institution can be proud: a level of success that builds the collective and maintains pride on all levels of the institution's bearings, an institutional legacy that lives beyond its time.

Unfortunately, in our experience, higher education has been much better at engaging explicit rather than implicit processes to produce educational outcomes for its students, including within its diversity mission.

An example from one of our authors was an interactive seminar where two psychologists not only lectured on the social science research behind implicit bias, but also led the audience through an interactive audience-participation demonstration of how the classic experiments on implicit bias were run in the psychology laboratory. It was compelling, especially since the group showed the basic implicit bias result in the live demonstration even after being educated academically about the topic.

In terms of direct-action activities, implicit bias workshops for everyone are a good start. While one could run multiple workshops, center the training in residence halls, or rely on general education or required diversity courses to do the training, that is not the point. The point is to get at the fundamental conditions that set up the implicit bias in the first place. If implicit bias is an unconscious, learned tendency that can come from a place of anxiety or fear of the "other," one way to break down barriers between groups is to encourage intercultural relations. The fear associated with connecting with groups you do not typically identify with does not come from bad experiences with another socio-cultural group, just the absence of experiences. There is a natural caution against venturing into the out-group from your in-group. Past the fear, though, cultural exchange lays down new experiences for students and higher education administrations. This foundation could alter the unconscious biases that exist in our minds and plague our societies.

CAN ONE BUILD IN-GROUP STRENGTH WITHOUT CULTIVATING OUT-GROUP DISRESPECT?

To continue this discussion, we return to some social neuroscience factors relating to in-group/out-group interaction. First, we must be aware of both our unconscious and conscious decision-making processes, or what Daniel Kahneman calls respectively the "fast thinking" process and the more deliberative "slow thinking" processes.[94] Second, we must be especially aware of unconscious decision-making processes, as failure to recognize bias can lead to greater division between groups – the subject of Joshua Green's recent book entitled, "Moral Tribes: Emotion, Reason, and the Gap Between Us and Them."[95]

A focus on unconscious decision-making leads us to focus on opportunities for experiential learning that lower barriers to the mixing of individuals with groups outside their own. We believe that such practices will create a more balanced education and a higher motivation for individual students to approach each other across group barriers.

A student completing her freshman year at the University at Albany, wrote a set of three blogs on the topic of entering unfamiliar groups of students.[96] In her blogs, she describes feeling anxiety upon entering a group that is not her own. Although she is from the South Asian country of Bangladesh, she does not completely identify with the largest Asian group on campus, dominated by students from China. Despite being part of the EOP program,[97] she notes feeling an internal tension in herself that comes when she initially moves into other campus groups, e.g. Latino/a or African American. Using what we term in the blog "conscious control," she works to control that social anxiety by making sure she enters the other group and accomplishes her personal diversity learning goal of crossing from one ethnic group to another, despite generating social anxiety caused by concerns about acceptance. Difficult though it may be to challenge her initial ways of thinking, she is explicitly trying to recalibrate her unconscious decision-making operations through new experiences.

The blog series ascribes the fear and anxiety of entering a new group to an emotion-related brain area that is called the amygdala, noting that the prefrontal cortex also plays a regulatory role.[98] In this neuroscience view, the prefrontal cortex functions in higher-level planning. The student has a clear plan to increase the diversity of interactions in her own college social experience. Natural social anxiety poses a hurdle, existing as a barrier to entry to other groups with unfamiliar behaviors, culture, food, and language. No one likes to look stupid or make mistakes, especially in front of new acquaintances. Of course, an open-minded group will welcome and teach the newcomer. But how do you know in advance if you will be welcomed?

The kind of ethnic group-spanning activity discussed in this blog provides a good foundation for universities to build upon. Institutions can encourage the formation of multicultural groups in many ways, from sororities (e.g. Mu Sigma Epsilon[99]) to deliberately diverse intramural sports teams organized by student life, or even a community service or arts activities that intentionally involve interaction across group lines. These are all examples of group-spanning activities with potentially powerful effects on the individual. The key is for the operation to involve diverse groups of individuals who share a purpose toward which all members can drive, for example, winning the intramural basketball match.[100] The result here is the cross-group friendships that develop out-group familiarity and break down implicit bias. The personal friendships that grow as you work together can counter the natural group tendency to exclude outsiders.

It takes a bit of courage to step into any new situation, whether it is a different group of people, whether across racial identification groups or gender barriers, as we have seen through the many ways women have challenged and continue to challenge the "old boys club." In the rise of the Black Lives Matter movement in the last few months, the United States has faced a reckoning of its entrenched systems of racial hierarchy. These issues are worthy of open discussion in and outside the classroom and courtroom – even where there is pushback.

In her 2017 book, *How Emotions Are Made,*[101] author Lisa Feldman Barrett argues that we can actively retrain our brains to work against biases through real-world experiences, for greater understanding of all those who make up our community. She holds that emotional responses are constructed over a lifetime as complex brain circuits make predictions of what will happen, check the result, and learn. She points out the role of language and learning in establishing basic emotions in childhood. Although the blogwriter mentioned above is an adult, Sarmin's example of a student who is trying to diffuse her social anxiety triggered by entering new groups operates in a similar way. Correction of those predictions through positive experiences lead to a modification of the emotional representations and to the activation of networks of specific brain regions. The good news from neuroscience is that these brain networks are plastic, meaning that emotional reactions can be changed, albeit with effort, to reshape the emotions experienced. Said another way, we do not have to accept our biases as inherent and can work successfully to change them.

As colleges and universities should seek to create group-spanning student activities, the staff and administration should support them when they arise naturally. This is where Student Life operations can work closely and experientially with the students to leverage their power for administrator understanding.

WHAT ARE SOME EXAMPLES OF GROUP-SPANNING ACTIVITIES FOR STUDENTS FROM DIVERSE BACKGROUNDS?

Here are a few examples to illustrate where universities can improve:

- Groups of students from diverse backgrounds may form a team around a common purpose, identity, or cultural traditions. e.g. Fuerza Latina, Jamaican Student Association, and other connections created between departments.

- Groups within a particular demographic that are linked to a profession, e.g. the nation-wide Student National Medical Association and the undergraduate campus-based Minority Association of Pre-Medical/Pre-Health Students.[102] Here, the university can combine the work of its Diversity Office with its pre-medical career services or pre-professional advising. Many other groups exist in STEM and other domains in which underserved populations need to be better represented.

- Centers that are dedicated to student group spanning activities, like the Center for Ethnic, Racial, and Religious Understanding at Queens College,[103] CUNY.

Department and administrators play a key role in promoting undergraduate involvement, making sure that students are mentored and developed personally as they also further the university's mission. Committing to and establishing a social justice mission of the college or university may be the most powerful way to build, campus-wide, a diversity understanding between students. Institutional mission is a common motivator that can band together many groups, particularly students and systems in higher education.

When students feel they are being "acted upon" instead of being "joined with," the educational process from taking place is disrupted. It is similar to someone talking at you instead of speaking with you. The former is demonstrated in the traditional fact-and-theories curriculum already in place before their students' arrival. It is found in the large lecture-based classroom where the professor is the "sage on the stage" and does not interact much with the average student. Experiential teaching about diversity, reducing implicit bias, and navigating in-group/out-group dynamics are valuable group-based diversity learning methods that educational institutions may not have yet fully applied.[104] We hope that our book's focus on diversity in higher education marks a turning point campus embodiment of the diversity mission that many institutions say they want to teach.

INDIVIDUAL AGENCY: SELF-HANDICAPPING AND STEREOTYPE THREAT

We will now review stereotype threat and self-handicapping to reemphasize that a lack of confidence can undermine individual student performance and create conditions ripe for a downward academic spiral. While these phenomena take place within the minds of individuals, they are heavily influenced by groups through unconscious decision-making. This dynamic is especially true if the group with which an individual identifies is subject to a societally-ingrained stereotype that they are not able, not equal, and not likely to succeed, as in Rachel's story of self-handicapping (Chapter 3) regarding women in the medical field or Agata's story of stereotype threat (Chapter 6) as an immigrant and non-native English speaker in an American high school. The effect on the individual is powerful. Microaggressions, like when Rachel was told that women would be better off as nurses than as doctors, have the capacity to undermine an individual's agency and self-worth.

These doubts extend to issues of identity and self-attributions of strength and weakness that are culturally ascribed to a group. As discussed in Chapter 6, stereotype threat preys on self-perceived weakness, as in Claude Steele's 1995 findings on Black students and standardized testing. Steele later wrote an important book in 2010 on the subject, called "Whistling Vivaldi: How Stereotypes Affect Us and What We Can Do" that showed how bias affected everyday life of minority students.[105] Because Steele was also the Provost at Berkeley and Columbia Universities, he had special expertise on universities and the broad application of stereotype threat to higher education. He and others also described many mitigation strategies,[106] including:

- **Teaching students about biases.** Students cannot make progress on inherent biases until they are made aware of them. Knowing about the harm that microaggressions can cause, as we discussed in Chapter 1, may make people more careful in their use of words.
- **Persuading students that they can change themselves through disciplined work and self-discovery**. This can help students develop skills they have not yet tapped into. The

belief that one can improve with work and study is called a Growth Mindset and it is critical to accomplishment.[107]

- **Creating self-affirmation combined with institutional affirmation.** Through the endorsement of the "growth mindset," institutions can persuade students that their apparent intelligence can be increased through learning. This mindset shift may work better when individuals are supported by a group that believes in itself as individuals and collectively, as in the example of EOP. But this role can also be filled by faculty mentoring, coach encouragement in an athletic team, and other student group advisors.

- **Implementing a system of matching students with role models or older peer mentors** whose identity markers match those of students who are displaying signals of stereotype threat or self-handicapping. Beyond professors and coaches, the population of graduate students and older undergraduate classmates have important potential as organic role models that often goes unspoken.

- **Directing students toward work and other experiential activities where they can succeed,** including internships (paid and unpaid), study abroad, service-learning, undergraduate research, and so on. These will be discussed more in-depth below.

These types of approaches develop the student's self-confidence and that compliments the development of professional agency from career related internships that in turn leads to success after college graduation.

STUDENT LEADERSHIP: HOW DO STUDENT LEADERSHIP EXPERIENCES SUPPORT DIVERSITY EDUCATION AND WHAT CAN ADMINISTRATORS DO TO CONTINUE TO IMPROVE UPON THIS EFFECT?

The first step is simple and generally practiced. Upon stepping foot on campus, each and every student should, and often does, encounter a real-world or virtual welcoming festival featuring a myriad of student groups, clubs, and organizations. If the new student finds and expresses an interest in a student organization, whether it be soccer, biology research, chess club, or something else, a system should be in place to exchange contact information. Soon after, a welcome message should come to that student from the group with an ask to get involved further or with relevant dates of programming and events. Many students report that the simple act of being invited to join a student group changed their college experience. This contact should be student-to-student, allowing existing diversity to be naturally represented among the current students.

Colleges and universities do pretty well attracting and retaining student involvement in leadership activities. But we also want to consider the ways in which they do not succeed, such as unequal funding allocated to different clubs and groups. We note that student athletic activities often get significant funding directly from the university and they can often generate revenue through ticket sales. Departments within a university are often funded on the basis of their ability to attract majoring students and fill courses. Smaller student clubs and groups do not have these same advantages, but they do indirectly generate revenue by helping institutions hold onto their students. We would like to acknowledge their role in student success and developing institutional cohesion and the mentors who support them. This effect is particularly true where it pertains to supporting student diversity on campus, as students from minority backgrounds face greater barriers to retention and graduation.

Orientation leaders and resident hall assistants are tasked with learning the interests of each student in their charge. This information is then passed on to and organized by the supervising staff, and later used to cultivate an enriching campus life for each new student. If the institution has an adequate electronic system of tracking student interest and connecting them with clubs and student groups, the operation is much more effective for all students, but particularly for new freshmen from first-generation and/or underprivileged backgrounds. Of course, ideally, the club president or membership officer will be proactive in recruiting them, as well. Their job is to make sure that everyone feels welcome to join every organization.

As students grow in their chosen organizations, they will be looked up to for guidance and support, which may ultimately put them in a critical role of leadership. Regardless of whether that now-experienced student has any interest in holding an official leadership role in the group, their knowledge and understanding of the organization will shine through. At the very least, they will be held in higher regard, giving them an even greater sense of belonging. Even when students are content simply being part of an organization and not pursuing leadership positions, they are accessing a great opportunity to both learn from their in- and out-group peers, as well as gain experiential knowledge, including a variety of possible soft skills (organization, emotional intelligence) and hard skills (learning a new language or computer program) that can be useful for their educational and career paths.

Colleges and universities typically hold leadership training programs for their emerging student leaders. Social integration in general is clearly crucial to a student's feeling that they matter at their institution. Irrespective of whether that integration manifests itself in student government, as in Marc's story, on the playing field, or elsewhere, leadership development in student groups effectively offered students a gateway to experiential learning and critical relationships that will sustain them.

A Community College Survey of Student Engagement (CCSSE) publication in 2009 found direct links between student engagement and student retention and graduation rates.[108] Specifically, relationships forged outside of the classroom are often of a deeper and more meaningful nature that is consequential to a successful student experience. We want to mention that although student-to-student interactions are very important, faculty interactions outside the classroom are also known to be critical. Yet the CCSSE report notes that 42% of part-time faculty members at community colleges, who teach most of the courses, spend no time at all working to advise or develop their students. While there are deeper issues at play there, student leadership opportunities can help compensate. Leaders from all walks of life play an important role in inspiring students and helping them feel included and heard on campus.

The educational system has undergone a debate about the benefits of an active learning movement in the classroom or "guide on the side" approach to teaching. We believe more of this direct collaboration between professors and students is deeply needed.

STUDENT LEADERSHIP: HOW STUDENT LEADERS REPRESENT AND SERVE THE DIVERSITY OF THE STUDENT BODY

You can be a leader in your classroom or in your social group. From elected leadership in the student government to club presidents to behind the scenes leaders, leadership takes varied forms. This last form of behind the scenes leadership is sometimes called "citizen leadership" – a type of informal leadership, in contrast to formal or elected leadership. When citizen leadership echoes the spirit of the group, it can be very powerful. This kind of leadership was discussed in Chapter 2 with Beny's organizing around faculty diversity.

Here, Beny stepped up in the conversation about how professors are chosen and why there are not more faculty of color in his university (and frankly in most universities). He noted that the process by which professors are selected may be well-known to department faculty but is something of a mystery to most students. Having identified that most professors in his Philosophy department did not reflect his identity, Beny developed a strong interest in understanding and promoting faculty of color in the university. Because he believed students needed to know why the proportion of minority faculty (9%) was not closer to the proportion of minority students (35%) at the University at Albany[109], he worked with his contacts in the student government and asked the administration to create a roundtable exchange to discuss the lack of diversity in hiring. A student does not need to be formally elected as a student government president to show leadership. Beny showed here informal, yet powerful student leadership. He lead from his authentic experience as a student, engaging in the direct collaboration that is so necessary to change. He leveraged his formal leadership position as a Student Government Senator to create an opportunity for citizen leadership not explicitly connected with his responsibilities as Senator.

While the University Strategic Plan had included a focus on increasing faculty diversity, Beny's efforts as a student leader furthered that goal in a way that brought the needs and interests of the student body into the discussion. As an administrator who attended the roundtable, one of us (Stellar) observes that it was eye-opening in two ways. First, it broadened students' understanding of the difficulties of recruiting a diverse and inclusive faculty that adequately reflects a diverse student body. Second, it enhanced the students' and the administration's understanding of each other in striving together to accomplish that task.

Both Chapter 2 and Chapter 5 discuss how student leadership combines the power of the group with the agency of each individual. This combination illustrates the way that university efforts, student efforts, and diversity education can intersect. There are many opportunities for students to be leaders in college, not only in the student government, but in other clubs and organizations found on and off campus. Some students even start new organizations, often around a service mission, like tutoring students at a local high school.

Student leadership can itself promote learning about diversity, and there is a great deal that can be learned about agency from experiential activities. Returning to the roundtable example, the experience of a discussion that brought students, faculty, and administrators closer together engages *all* students by reinforcing that their needs are valid and valued. This results in benefits for the university, such as increased student retention and the building of a graduating class who become alumni ambassadors by spreading word of their positive experiences in college. Opportunities like these give students of color a reason to cheer their university on. Student inclusion in these forward-looking conversations may provide powerful motivation to overcome self-handicapping and stereotype threat – and even drive them to later join the university as faculty themselves.

MENTORING ACROSS AGE, GENDER, ETHNICITY, AND RACE

The common conception of college as large lecture classes imparting facts and theories ignores an important reality of the college experience – the faculty themselves as mentors. Many faculty members actively choose to work in a university because they want to interact with students, as well as pursue scholarship in their fields. When faculty invest in their students, an individual student and their teacher can greatly benefit, even if the age, gender, ethnicity, and race do not overlap. In order for any faculty member to become a mentor to a student, a bond has to develop. It has to be organic, natural, and based on the understanding that the faculty member has developed of the student by listening to that individual and understanding their culture. Usually, it is the student who listens respectfully to the faculty member given the age, expertise, and institutional role difference. When both sides listen and the natural interests of the two people overlap, powerful mentorship can occur.

Faculty mentoring may begin as educational and career advising, but once a relationship is built, professors can provide support on more personal matters such as overcoming racism, sexism, or where the student feels inadequate due to youth and lack of experience. Mentors also help their students to overcome what has been termed "imposter syndrome," whereby a person, possibly even a highly qualified one, compares themselves to others and doubts their abilities.[110] This syndrome can affect people of all ages. The lack of agency that results from a lack of confidence can be insidious and lead to inadequate career exploration (e.g. internships that are not done early enough in the college career or failure to bond with a faculty member who can write recommendation letters). Another common problem is aiming too low in jobs or applications for further education. The combination of faculty status in the intellectual field and familiarity with the individual student can be a powerful factor in elevating the aspirations of a student for their own career. Many students may not have their families advocating for them, and a mentor can fill that role for them.

In order for a student to have a truly meaningful experience, it is necessary for them to build a network in their respective fields from within and outside of their tribe. That will prove beneficial when it comes to getting help on academically challenging material, as well as later when students begin to search for job and internship opportunities. Our experience has shown that having the chance to build rapport with faculty and staff is a chief benefit of involvement and helps with retention. As we saw in Chapter 5, Marc joined his college dean's Leadership Council during his sophomore year. In addition to helping to set the trajectory for one of the highest-ranked colleges for public affairs in the country, he points out that he networked with and built a closer relationship with his professors. With that familiarity came a sense of duty to perform well and contribute to class discussions; what started as just another line on his resume evolved into a key contributor to graduating summa cum laude. What began as something for himself turned into fighting for something for all students on campus. Marc served as a role model for the Jewish community he grew up in, in particular, but just as his ambitions as a leader were grounded in providing a voice to groups like his, he also strove to work with and extend that opportunity to other communities. At a diverse university, being a student leader is about serving that diversity.

Beny grew from mentorship experiences with both faculty of color at the University and in his work with various members of the administration, due to his familiarity with them as a member of student government. But, as he says in Chapter 2, perhaps the greatest mentoring opportunity came from the Speaker of the New York State Assembly with whom Beny interned over the summer and that then led to a full spring semester SUNY internship in the Speaker's office. Beny related how important it was for him that the

Speaker himself was from a minority background, from the same part of New York City in which Beny grew up, and so understood Beny's own upbringing and cultural background. It is exactly this type of symbiotic mentorship that having a more diverse faculty at a university or college could allow more students to benefit from, including the additional educational and career opportunities it has the potential to unlock.

Student success is often a combination of the opportunities you can access and your agency as an individual. Part of the theme of this book is recognizing the systemic inequalities that reduce those opportunities for students who are not part of the majority culture - like Rachel as an aspiring female premedical student, Beny as a Latino philosophy major from the Bronx, and Agata as a Polish immigrant and non-native English speaker making it in college. From their stories, we learn that the personal agency that is developed in student groups and activities, from faculty mentoring, and in the classroom is critical to building leaders and fostering diversity learning. It is vital for students to become involved in and continue with an experience, opportunity, or connection long enough to see the fruits of their labor. The importance of this persistence cannot be overstated; it makes up a large part of the "behind the scenes" growth that is integral to the goals of experiential education.

THE VALUE OF STUDYING ABROAD IN HELPING STUDENT UNDERSTANDING OF DIVERSITY

Alongside other experiential education activities, study abroad builds students' individual agency by expanding their frames of reference. We return to study abroad here because of its immersive nature and the illuminating different perspectives on cultures that students gain. Despite the vast and in some ways unquantifiable benefits it brings, study abroad can pose financial barriers, particularly to students from a lower socioeconomic background and/or minority status. According to the American Council on Education, currently, less than 5% of all enrolled U.S. college and university students participate in study abroad, a subset that is not representative of the broad diversity on today's campuses.[111] The Senator Paul Simon Study Abroad Program Act is a competitive grant program for higher education institutions to expand these opportunities to all at the federal level.[112] Universities can and should make grant and scholarship information widely available, but currently existing funding opportunities do not suffice to expand access for all of the students who are interested in studying abroad. This is a major area where universities with fundraising capabilities can apply themselves to offset that barrier.

Most people in the United States talk about studying abroad as getting students out of their comfort zones and into other cultures that differ in language, customs, and viewpoints. Study abroad has become a major offering at colleges and universities over the last few decades to the point that, today, if an institution does not have a vigorous study abroad program, it contracts with an outside organization to provide options or faces a deficit in attracting students. Study abroad confers a breadth of experience that the students value and allows institutions to meet their objectives for educational breath that cannot quite be achieved at home.

There are some alternatives to the traditional overseas experiences that may be easier for universities to fund. Consider expanding access to shorter academic or volunteer trips of one to two weeks that take place during school holidays rather than semester-long programs. Service-based missions and exchanges provide a strong opportunity to build both hard and soft skills both generally and within a student's specific field, such as health with Global Brigades[113] or in engineering with Engineers without Borders.[114] Take as another example the opportunity to "study abroad at home," whereby a New Yorker spends a month (or more) in Alabama, and vice versa.[115] This provides a great way to compare and contrast the experience of growing up on different sides of the same country (as well as to find common ground) and does not require any particular language skills, which could make it more accessible to a wider range of students.

In places where there are large collections of ethnic enclaves, like major cities, domestic service-learning programs can have some of these benefits of cross-cultural immersion that could be useful to diverse student populations. For example, in Queens, New York, students have their choice of dense communities in which to study, including Chinese, Greek, Egyptian, Caribbean, Bukharan Jewish, and many more. This is a great opportunity for students to expand on and improve a non-native language for their professional and personal skill set. International students also offer a unique cross-cultural group with which students of United States origin can interact without even leaving their campus.

Wherever study "abroad" takes place, students develop and deepen their bond with their college by being its representative or ambassador. They do not only explain the culture of the United States to students from other countries, they explain their institution. This particular institutional dynamic is often under-leveraged by the college or university.

Co-author Chloe' considers her former on-campus job as a Writing Tutor in the Queens College Writing Center to be her most important experience with diversity.[116] Having grown up Jewish in a generally white, Roman Catholic, and affluent hometown, she craved the opportunity to learn about new cultures in university. She was inspired by the many international students who came from abroad to study in their non-native language, and what is more, *to write essays in it.* From her first Bangladeshi tutee who was a Subway employee and asked her to explain how he could distinguish between when the word "hot" means temperature hot or spicy, the Japanese master's student who taught her how to properly slurp ramen, and the Saudi Arabian exchange student who brought her traditional coffee made with saffron, Chloe' learned about other cultures, including different ways of relating to and speaking with people who grew up outside the U.S. She had the privilege to study abroad twice in college (both times with the help of scholarships and grants), whereby one month in Greece led to a spike in confidence that allowed her to spend six months in Israel. She went on to receive a Fulbright grant to teach English in the Czech

Republic, which stretched into a four-year period after graduation. After growing through all these experiences, she now counts the improvement of diversity and cross-cultural understanding among her most important personal and career goals.

Like-minded students from all walks of life at the university surely have a lot to contribute, so how can we leverage experiences like Chloe's on campus? After all, 5% is a small number of students, but that experience can be expanded to a larger audience given the right efforts. After returning from study abroad, Chloe' was invited to an event where she and other students who had recently returned from studying abroad gave presentations about their experiences to other students and faculty. This is a good start and we recommend expanding returned students' roles on campus. For example, they might host a series of presentations, diversity workshops, "Culture Cafés," or other events that feature a diverse range of participants and experiences (it is crucial not to feature abroad experiences from only one region). Universities can create a buddy system between former study abroad students with those who are interested in similar cultural, academic, or career experiences.

WHAT ABOUT INTERNATIONAL STUDENTS?

Colleges can match former study abroad students with new international student mentees to help them adapt to campus life. In the long term, they can try to cultivate a robust student exchange whereby students who have benefited from abroad experiences can host those who study on their campus. International students often share similar experiences of stereotype threat, implicit bias, and being on the receiving end of microaggressions and other forms of social conduct that can separate groups. Chloe' attests to reading more than one essay in which the international student writer grappled with expressing these difficult issues in their non-native language. Opening to the diverse populations of both international and local students an engaging and empowering forum in which to bond over their common experiences could ultimately give them greater agency to combat the issues they face in the United States.

There is huge potential to translate study abroad into an experience from which all students can take something away, running the gamut from cultural trivia to new clubs to long-term out-group bonding. Ideally, international students will find a stronger feeling of belonging within the host community. Meanwhile, the university benefits from an ever-growing community of cultural ambassadors.

BUILDING COMMUNITY AND CONNECTIONS THAT EXTEND BEYOND GRADUATION DAY

For most people in the United States, it is likely that their college years will be one of the greatest growth environments of their lives. From outside the college or university, there is often an illusion that students are exclusively under the institution's guidance from faculty, Student Life staff, administration, and other components of the campus community. But that is only for a part of the student's time: most of the time, students are with each other. Indeed, that interaction is one of the great joys of college, especially if the student is able to live on campus and thereby partake in after-hours activities that add to their intellectual and cultural growth.

We have gone over many ways to enhance implicit learning through diversity on college campuses, including through the implementation of programs like EOP, widening the range of group-spanning activities, working with professors to affirm student learning, working with student leaders to serve the needs of a diverse student body, and providing mentorship and study abroad opportunities. The status-quo tradition is for students to "be educated" and thus be "acted upon." Yet for truly transformative education to take place, students must take the lead - and administrators must not only allow but encourage them - to become a joint partner in the educational process.

Both in- and out-of-the-classroom experiences can be dynamic, and what has been is not what has to be. It is up to you to take the facts-and-theories approach of classical higher education and apply it to improving the system. Professors and administrators may have their ingrained rules and methods, but we want to remind students and administrators both that the student body is a dynamic indicator of innovative ideas and a collective of change agents.

The ultimate underlying goal is a return to the meaning of education in the first place - in fact, why higher education exists at all. University culture that emphasizes a partnership between hard and soft skills (explicit and implicit learning) can help students later become well-adapted, productive, and confident members of the workforce. Students whose educational framework promotes collaboration across the student body will then be able to adapt to a future workplace with coworkers from all walks of life. With education, the idea goes, you expand your consciousness and understand your world better. Through learning about diversity in the context of a diverse world, we learn more about and understand each other better. This makes us well-adapted and productive members of a world community.

If you are reading this right now, you have the ability to actively work against your biases through participation in and expansion of experiential opportunities. This means not only accepting that we all have biases, but also taking up the lifelong challenge of interrogating our beliefs about "the other." It means we must resolve to step outside of our comfort zones and learn from each other, continuously. And this is what it is all about. The end goal is to create "transformative spaces where people of all races, ethnicities, passions, and abilities can come together and thrive.

We know it is not that simple. It takes a lot of hard work. But it begins with the aspirational – recognizing that we will get a lot farther in this world if we try to understand each other, treat each other with respect, and work together. This is exactly the "learning through doing with reflection on that doing" that our stories revolve around. The data supports this: Not only does diversity improve our society, the experiential approach works. With this in mind, you can work to connect your campus community by tapping into student diversity, creating a space where students feel comfortable being uniquely themselves, and providing the opportunities where students share with each other, learn from each other, and grow together. If students see each other as a united group made up of many smaller, united groups, then we have made huge strides towards both individual and collective student success. Learning these patterns while in college can then naturally extend to life after graduation. Ultimately, when we work together to raise up all members of society, we raise the level of economic mobility.

It is powerful when students realize they are not just joining a club – they are learning how to network, collaborate with people of all backgrounds, and deepen their intellectual growth. Administrators are not just improving the reputation of their schools; they are increasing economic opportunities for everyone.

Higher education is the beauty and struggle of coming into your own as an intellectual being. Students are there now. Administrators will hopefully never stop learning. This work is hard, but fruitful. The earlier you start and the more you work at it, the more natural it will come to feel.

APPENDIX

Brief biographical notes to the reader from each co-author

STELLAR

This is an unusual book. It is co-authored by young people with important felt experience and authentic voices on this topic. One of them, me, comes from a different background. I am not a recent graduate. I grew up long ago in a peaceful majority-culture family with adequate resources. I became a professor of neuroscience, first at Harvard, and then Northeastern Universities, took on senior academic leadership positions at Northeastern and to the public universities, at Queens College CUNY and then University at Albany SUNY. There, something happened.

While I was developing and publishing my first lay-oriented book with IdeaPress on experiential education, I was also interacting with the highly diverse student populations of these two public institutions. I realized that while I wanted to help these students grow in college, I was not prepared by my own history to understand their experiences well enough. That led me to invite many of them to write about it on my experiential education blog,[117] to talk to me as best they could about their challenges and development, and eventually to come together over a few years and write this book.

It is perhaps trite to say, but life is a journey and it is so for its entire duration. My ongoing journey on this topic of diversity has been informed by scholars, but more importantly, it has been led by the gracious and heartfelt sharing of students, faculty, and staff – and particularly of my co-authors. I feel lucky to be among them all and to have them as teachers. Read the book and you will see what I mean.

MARTINEZ

A gentle force and a fighter towards societal justice, Chrisel's political philosophy is based on eradicating the systems that lead to economic disparities found amongst most Black, Latino and other minorities. Her Dominican roots ground her in the ideals of liberation and joy, while her Harlem haven provides her with longstanding motivation towards the fight for reform. As a graduate of the University at Albany, SUNY, Chrisel graduated with a pseudo-degree in Economics and Leadership Development. Her various positions as a student advocate merited her a postgraduate placement in the Coro Fellowship Program in public affairs. This 9-month leadership development experience supported her desires in understanding the political depths of New York City, and thus our nation. As an aspiring lawyer she looks to laws of God to influence her moral compass and worldly framework. As a leading editor in this project, Chrisel encourages us to speak our deepest truths and to listen with compassion.

EGGAN

Branden (Brandy) Eggan, PhD is an assistant professor of anatomy and physiology and neuroscience at Siena College. She comes from a background in addiction research and behavioral neuroscience but her current research focuses on themes shown in this book: the importance of diversity in higher education as well as barriers to success faced by specific underrepresented groups.

Additionally, Brandy is active in many undergraduate and high school research programs focused on motivating these students into research and STEM careers. Mentorship is greatly important to her and she strives to serve as a role model and passionate advocate for students who feel their voices are not heard. At Albany Medical College Brandy also works with medical students and the national BNGAP (Building the Next Generation of Academic Physicians) board to advocate for URM students pursuing a career in academic medicine, where diversity and mentorship are lacking, following the completion of their graduate degree.

WEISER

Chloe' Skye Weiser is an ESL teacher, international copy-writer, and avid traveler who has lived in the USA, Israel, Czech Republic, and Denmark (so far). She was a 2014-2015 Fulbright English Teaching Assistant in the Czech Republic. Her experiences as a Writing Tutor at Queens College first sparked her passion for intercultural communication and fostering cultural understanding. A self-dubbed "informal anthropologist," she explores language, culture, and the expat experience on her travel blog, Chlohemian.

POY

Beny Poy currently works for the National Association of Latino Elected and Appointed Officials (NALEO) Educational Fund as a Program Coordinator. Beny's role involves advocating for the full engagement of the nation's 2nd largest demographic, Latinos, in all civic and political processes in a strictly nonpartisan manner. Beny's work focuses on Latino electoral participation as well as Latino inclusion in the decennial census and state redistricting process. Most recently, Beny led a statewide latinx coalition that successfully advocated for the appointment of the first and only latina to serve on New York State's Independent Redistricting Commission.

EAGER

Rachel Eager now works in Health Information Technology where she manages programs to get providers connected to New York's Health Information Exchange. On the side, she pursues a part-time

Masters in Healthcare Administration from Columbia University. In May 2018, Rachel graduated with her honors degree in Biochemistry and Molecular Biology with minors in Political Science and Women's Gender and Sexuality Studies from the University at Albany. The professors at the university in so many ways helped to grow her as a person and increase her curiosity in learning. Although she originally wished to pursue medicine, her internships and professors pushed her towards her passion for health policy and health technology. Rachel grew up and stayed in the Albany area for her undergraduate degree but recently relocated to New York City. In her free time, Rachel enjoys running, finding new gluten-free foodie spots, having a wonderful time with friends, traveling the world, and enjoying a beautiful beach day. In addition, she likes to find new hiking spots throughout New York during the summer and spending time on the lake with her family and friends.

COHEN

Marc Cohen became Chief of Staff at the Greater Rochester Chamber of Commerce in December 2018. Marc directly oversees government relations, legislative affairs, and advocacy, and is the primary policy advisor to the Rochester Chamber's CEO, Robert J. Duffy.

Additionally, Marc is charged with identifying process improvement opportunities, best practices, and cost-saving measures, working with partners to promote and enhance regional workforce and economic development efforts, serving as Mr. Duffy's and the Rochester Chamber's representative at outside forums and on community work groups, and overseeing the daily operations of the executive office.

Prior to joining the Rochester Chamber, Marc served as a Trustee for the State University of New York and as President of the SUNY Student Assembly, elected to represent the 1.4 million students across SUNY's 64 campuses. During his time with SUNY, Marc worked on issues including food insecurity, college access and affordability, diversity and inclusion, and mental health.

Marc grew up in Amherst, NY, and graduated *summa cum laude* from the University at Albany before completing his Master of Public Administration from UAlbany's Rockefeller College.

BURAS

Agata was born in Poland and moved to New York as a teen. She began her interest in psychology and neuroscience at Queens College where she attended. She joined a laboratory focusing on neuroscience research, where she earned her publications and a research award. She also began working on a blog with Dr. Stellar and helping design and teach an undergraduate course at Queens College and, more recently, at the University at Albany. That work led to her participation in this book.

Agata believes that it is the similarities in our differences that brought the authors together to write this book. It is the product of hard work and a positive attitude. She hopes this book will help you, the reader, overcome your own personal struggles.

A big thank you to the people who supported her, parents, mentors, and best friend.

ENDNOTES

1. Jack, Anthony. **The Privileged Poor: How Elite Colleges Are Failing Disadvantaged Students.** Cambridge, MA: Harvard University Press, 2019.

2. Kendi, Ibram. **Stamped from the Beginning.** New York, NY: Bold Type Books, 2016.

3. Queens College CUNY and University at Albany SUNY

4. The recent strong social movement that is Black Lives Matter took off after this manuscript was submitted to the publisher but is naturally highly relevant to our topic.

5. In sociology and social psychology, an in-group is a social group to which a person psychologically identifies as being a member. By contrast, an out-group is a social group with which an individual does not identify (https://en.wikipedia.org/wiki/Ingroups_and_outgroups). Note: here and elsewhere when we cite references, particularly to popular media, we have reviewed the citation first.

6. Bertrand, M. & Mullainathan, S. **Are Emily and Greg more employable**

than Lakisha and Jamal? A field experiment on labor market discrimination. *The American Economic Review,* vol. 94, no. 4, 2003, pp. 991-1013.

7. Chambers, K., Onishi, K., and Fisher, C. **Infants learn phonotactic regularities from brief auditory experience.** *Cognition,* vol 87, 2003, pp B69-77. and Jusczyk, P., Luce, P., and Chares-Luce, J. **Infants' sensitivity to phonotactic patterns in the native language.** *Journal of Memory and Language,* vol. 33, no. 5, 1994, pp 630-645.

8. Sue, D.W. **Microaggressions in everyday life: Race, gender, and sexual orientation.** Hoboken, NJ, John Wiely & Sons Inc., 2010. Also see Hampson, Sarah. Derald Wing Sue on microaggression, the implicit racism minorities endure. July 2016: https://www.theglobeandmail.com/life/relationships/derald-wing-sue-on-microaggressions-racism/article30821500/.

9. Zuckerman, M, and Driver, R. "Telling Lies: Verbal and Nonverbal Correlates of Deception" in (Eds. Seligman, A. and Feldstein, S.) **Multichannel Integrations of Non Verbal Behavior,** Psychology Press, New York, NY. 1985, pp 129-144.

10. Kahneman, Daniel. **Thinking fast and slow.** New York: Farrar, Straus, and Giroux, 2011.

11. Simeon Sinek. **Start with why: How great leaders inspire everyone to take action.** New York, Penguin Group, 2009.

12. Bhargava, Rohit. **Likeconomics: The unexpected truth behind earning trust, influencing behavior, and inspiring action.** Hoboken, NJ, John Wiley & Sons, 2012.

13. Eagleman, David. **Incognito: The secret lives of the hidden brain.** New York: Knopf Doubleday Publishing Group, 2011.

14. Zak, Paul. Ted Talk: Trust, Morality, and Oxytocin. July 2011: https://www.ted.com/talks/paul_zak_trust_morality_and_oxytocin?language=en.

15. Galbally, M., Lewis, A.J., Van Ijzendoorm, M., and Permezel, M. **The role of oxytocin in mother-infant relations: A systematic review of human studies.** *Harv Rev Psychiatry,* vol 19(1), 2011, pp 1-14. Chambers, K., Onishi, K., and Fisher, C. **Infants learn phonotactic regularities from brief auditory experience.** *Cognition,* vol 87, 2003, pp B69-77.

16. Andrews, Julie. The scientific reason we all need more hugs. January

2019: https://www.theloop.ca/the-scientific-reason-we-all-need-more-hugs/.

17. Zhang, H., Gross, J., De Dreu, C., Ma, Y. **Oxytocin promotes coordinated out-group attack during intergroup conflict in humans.** *eLife,* vol 8, 2019, e40698.

18. Haidt, Jonathan. **The righteous mind: Why good people are divided by politics and religion.** New York, Random House, 2012.

19. Monroe, Carla. **Race and Colorism in Education (Routledge Research in Educational Equality and Diversity).** New York: Routledge, 2017.

20. Radzicki-McManus, Melanie. How empathy works. March 2017: https://science.howstuffworks.com/life/inside-the-mind/emotions/empathy3.htm.

21. Premack, D. &Woodruff, G. **Does the chimpanzee have a theory of mind?** *Behavioral and Brain Sciences*, vol. 1, no. 4, 1978, pp 515-526.

22. Gallese, V. & Goldman, A. **Mirror neurons and the simulation theory of mind-reading**. *Trends in Cognitive Sciences,* vol. 2, 1998, pp 493-501. and Iacoboni, M. **Imitation, Empathy, and Mirror Neurons**. *Annual Review of Psychology*, vol.60, 2009, pp 653-670.

23. Cooperative Education and Internship Association: https://www.ceiainc.org/about/history

24. Auld, Robert. **The cooperative education movement: Association of cooperative colleges**. *Journal of Cooperative Education,* vol. 8, 1972, pp. 24-27.

25. While there are many definitions of the co-curricular transcript at different institutions, we offer this one from BMCC: https://www.bmcc.cuny.edu/student-affairs/student-activities/cct/.

26. With an evolution from both industry and academics (https://en.wikipedia.org/wiki/T-shaped_skills), this T-shape concept seems to fit with the conscious/unconscious decision-making ideas already discussed.

27. Stellar, JR. **Education that Works: The Neuroscience of Building a more Effective Higher Education**. Ideapress, 2017.

28. Pinker, Steven. **The better angels of our nature: Why violence has declined**. New York: Penguin Publishing Group, 2011.

29. Eswaran, Vijay. The business case for diversity in the workplace is now

overwhelming. April 2019: https://www.weforum.org/agenda/2019/04/business-case-for-diversity-in-the-workplace/.

30. Fernandez, Manny. When Presidents Visited the South Bronx. October 2007: https://cityroom.blogs.nytimes.com/2007/10/05/when-presidents-visited-the-south-bronx/.

31. Gelinas, N. The Bronx is up: Devastated for decades, the borough has roared back - but pockets of poverty remain. December, 2016: https://www.city-journal.org/html/bronx-14182.html.

32. Authors note: We will return to EOP in Chapter 4 and Chapter 7 of this book.

33. One program at UMBC – Hansen, Sarah. UMBC launches PROMISE Academy with USM partners, to support diverse faculty in the biomedical sciences. December 2018: https://news.umbc.edu/umbc-launches-promise-academy-with-usm-partners-to-support-diverse-faculty-in-the-biomedical-sciences/.

34. Mahzarin Banaji profile: https://psychology.fas.harvard.edu/people/mahzarin-r-banaji and Anthony Greenwald profile: https://faculty.washington.edu/agg/.

35. Keith Payne, Laura Niemi, & John Doris. How to Think about Implicit Bias. March 2018: https://www.scientificamerican.com/article/how-to-think-about-implicit-bias/.

36. Malcolm Gladwell. **Blink: The Power of Thinking Without Thinking.** New York, NY, Back Bay Books. 2005.

37. Shankar Vedantam. **The Hidden Brain: How Our Unconscious Minds Elect Presidents, Control Markets, Wage Wars, and Save our Lives.** New York, NY, Random House Publishing Group, 2010.

38. Jesse Singal. Psychology's Racism Measuring Tool isn't up to the Job. January 2017: https://www.thecut.com/2017/01/psychologys-racism-measuring-tool-isnt-up-to-the-job.html.

39. Price, Joshua. **The effect of instructor race and gender on student persistence in STEM fields.** *Economics of Education Review,* vol. 29, 2010, pp 901-910. or Rask, Kevin N. and Bailey, Elizabeth M. **Are Faculty Role Models? Evidence from Major Choice in an Undergraduate Institution.** *Research in Economic Education,* vol. 33, 2002, pp 99-124.

40. Meyers, Ben. Where are the minority professors? February 2016: https://

www.chronicle.com/interactives/where-are-the-minority-professors. or Figlio, David. The importance of a diverse teaching force. November 2017: https://www.brookings.edu/research/the-importance-of-a-diverse-teaching-force/. or

Gershenson, Seth and Papageorge, Nicholas. The power of teacher expectations: How racial bias hinders student attainment. December 2018: https://www.educationnext.org/power-of-teacher-expectations-racial-bias-hinders-student-attainment/.

41. Ho, Phoebe. and Cherng, Hua-Yu Sebastian. **How far can the apple fall? Differences in teacher perceptions of minority and immigrant parents and their impact on academic outcomes.** *Social Science Research,* vol. 74, 2018, pp 132-145.

42. Cited previously in reference 28 and in a more recent article about the success of the UMBC Meyerhoff program: Hrabowski, Freeman A. and Henderson, Peter H. How undergraduate programs can boost minority success in medical school. January 2017: https://news.aamc.org/diversity/article/how-undergraduate-programs-boost-minority-success/.

43. Kang, Kelly. National center for science and engineering doctorate recipients from U.S. universities: 2017. December 2018: https://ncses.nsf.gov/pubs/nsf19301/data.

44. Zuckerman, M. and Tsai, F. **Costs of self-handicapping.** *J Personality,* vol 73(2), 2005, 411-442.

45. Sandberg, S. **Lean In: Women, Work and the Will to Lead.** New York, NY: Knopf Doubleday Publishing Group, 2013.

46. Aronson, J. and Steele, C. **Stereotypes and the fragility of academic competence, motivation, and self-concept (Ch. 24).** In *Handbook of Competence and Motivation* (Eds. Elliot and Dweck), The Guilford Press, NY, 2005 pp 436-456.

47. Note the brain reference to anterior cingulate cortex under mechanisms from: https://en.wikipedia.org/wiki/Stereotype_threat and Krendl, A.C., Richeson, J.A., Kelley, W.M., and Heatherton, T.F. **The negative consequences of threat: a functional magnetic resonance imaging investigation of the neural mechanisms underlying women's underperformance in math.** *Physiological Science,* vol. 18, no.2, 2008, pp 168-175.

48. Glicksman, Eve. A first; Women outnumber men in 2017 entering medical school class. December 2017: https://news.aamc.org/medical-educa-

tion/article/first-women-outnumber-men-2017-entering-medical-s/.

49. Jones, Julia Hughes. **The secret history of weeds: What women need to know about their history**. Booklocker.com Publishing, 2009.

50. Carli Linda L. **Gender and social influence**. *Journal of social issues,* vol. 57, no. 4, 2001, pp 725-741.

51. Cohn, Laura. This female exec changed her name to a man's to get a job. Should you? June 2016: http://fortune.com/2016/06/08/name-bias-in-hiring/.

52. Study cited in Chapter 1, reference number 6.

53. Moss-Racusin, C.A., Dovidio, J.F., Brescoll, V.L., Graham, M.J., and Handelsman, J. **Science faculty's subtle gender bias favors male students**. *PNAS*, vol. 109, no. 41, 2012, pp 16474-16479.

54. Steele, C and Aronson, J. **Stereotype threat and the intellectual test performance of African Americans**. *Journal of Personality and Social Psychology,* vol. 69, 1995, pp 797-811.

55. Reid, S., and Steller J.S. A view on student diversity and STEM education from someone raised in Jamaica. March, 2020: http://otherlobe.com/a-view-on-student-diversity-and-stem-education-from-someone-raised-in-jamaica/.

56. At first, many universities were resistant to the idea that undergraduate students could engage in research with faculty. That changed with the Undergraduate Research Opportunity Program at MIT in the late 1969. Now, research universities and even colleges brag about their programs and see this activity as a critical way to build student education, as well as attract them in the first place (https://en.wikipedia.org/wiki/Undergraduate_research), or (https://libraries.mit.edu/mithistory/institute/offices/undergraduate-research-opportunities-program-urop/).

57. Del Cid, Jessica. **The American dream: An illusion or reality for Latino immigrants**. *Senior Thesis: Liberty University,* 2011.

58. McLanahan, Sara. The consequences of single motherhood. December 2001: https://prospect.org/health/consequences-single-motherhood/.

59. Pacheco, C.M. et al. **Homes of low income minority families with asthmatic conditions have increased condition issues**. *Allergy and Asthma Proceedings,* vol. 35, no. 6, 2014, pp 467-474.

60. Spanish Harlem's word for local deli owners.

61. Spanish Harlem's word for the male and female neighbors in the community.

62. American Psychological Association: https://www.apa.org/pi/ses/resources/publications/education.

63. Abdul-Alim, Jamal. Graduate defends orientation program accused of hazing. November 2016: https://diverseeducation.com/article/89121/

64. University at Albany's Educational Opportunities Program: https://www.albany.edu/eop/.

65. For information about the Coro New York Leadership Center reference the following: https://coronewyork.org/.

66. Shakur, Tupac. **The rose that grew from concrete.** November 1999: https://www.goodreads.com/quotes/52680-did-you-hear-about-the-rose-that-grew-from-a

67. Big-fish-little-pond effect: https://en.wikipedia.org/wiki/Big-fish%E2%80%93little-pond_effect, or Marsh, H.W., and Parker, J.W. **Determinants of student self-concept. Is it better to be a relatively large fish in a small pond even if you don't swim as well?** *Journal of Personality and Social Psychology,* vol 47(1), 1984, pp 213-231.

68. Gladwell, Malcolm. **David and Goliath: Underdogs, Misfits, and the Art of Battling Giants.** New York, Back Bay Books, 2013.

69. For more information on the State University at New York System: https://www.suny.edu.

70. Tajfel, H. **Individuals and groups in social psychology.** *British Journal of Social and Clinical Psychology,* vol. 18(2), 1979, pp 183-190. Also see https://en.wikipedia.org/wiki/Henri_Tajfel

71. Pinker, S. **The village effect: How face-to-face contact makes us healthier, happier, and smarter.** New York: Spiegel & Garu, 2014.

72. Nagasawa, M., Kikusui, T., Onaka, T., Ohta, M. **Dog's gaze at its owner increases owner's urinary oxytocin during social interaction.** *Hormones and Behavior,* vol. 55, 2009, pp 434-441.

73. Feldman, R. **Oxytocin and social affiliations in humans.** *Hormones and Behavior,* vol. 61(3), 2012, pp 380-391.

74. Shalvi, S., De. Dreu, C. **Oxytocin promotes group-serving dishonesty.**

PNAS, vol. 111, 2014, pp 5503-5507.

75. Sheng, F. Liu, Y., Zhou, B., Zhou, W., Han, S. **Oxytocin modulates the racial bias in neural responses to others' suffering.** *Biological Psychology,* vol. 92, 2013, pp 380-386.

76. Osterman, K.F. **Students' need for belonging in the school community.** *Review of Educational Research,* vol. 70(3), 2000, pp 323-367.

77. Asch, S. **Studies of independence and conformity: I. A minority of one against a unanimous majority.** *Psychological Monographs: General and Applied,* vol. 70(9), 1956, pp 1-70.

78. see footnote 67.

79. Castro, Jason. You have a hive mind. March 2012: https://www.scientificamerican.com/article/you-have-a-hive-mind/.

80. Seeley, T. The lives of bees: The untold story of the honey bee in the wild. Princeton, NJ, Princeton University Press, 2019.

81. Singh, Shalini and Stellar, James. The social brain and the experiential education in and out of the classroom. June 2014: http://otherlobe.com/papers/the-social-brain-and-the-experiential-education-in-and-out-of-the-classroom/.

82. As discussed in the text, "flipped-hybrid" is a reference to two aspects of a course. "Hybrid" refers to the fact that some of the work is done in on-line exercises outside of class and therefore the in-class meeting time is reduced. "Flipped" refers to the fact that during in-class meetings, some class time was devoted to guided discussion of content material rather than standard lecture. This course featured both with the idea of deepening student engagement with the material.

83. Buras, Agata and Stellar, James. Bringing experiential education techniques to the "flipped" classroom, undergraduate-professor partnership, and student engagement. July 2015: http://otherlobe.com/papers/bringing-experiential-education-techniques-to-the-flipped-classroom-undergraduate-professor-partnership-and-student-engagement/.

84. See footnote 55. Steele, C and Aronson, J. **Stereotype threat and the intellectual test performance of African Americans.** *Journal of Personality and Social Psychology,* vol. 69, 1995, pp 797-811.

85. Krendl, A.C., Richeson, J.A., Kelley, W.M., Heatherton, T.F. **The negative consequences of threat: A functional magnetic resonance imaging**

investigation of neural mechanisms underlying women's underperformance in math. *Psychological Science,* vol. 19(2), 2008, pp 168-175.

86. The role of the amygdala has been classically in fear, but newer thinking challenges any such simple linking of an emotion with a specific brain area. For more information see: Feldman, Lisa Barrett. **How emotions are made.** Boston: Houghton, Mifflin, Harcourt Publishing, 2017.

87. Delong, Matt and Winter, Dale. **Learning to teach and teaching to learn mathematics; Resources for professional development.** Washington, DC: Mathematical Association of America, 2001.

88. Rosenthal, R. **The "file drawer problem" and the tolerance for null results.** *Psychological Bulletin,* vol. 86, no. 3, 1979, pp 638-641.

89. For a recent review see: Spencer, S.J., Logel, C., and Davies, P.G. **Stereotype Threat.** *Annual Review of Psychology,* 67, 2016, pp 415-437.

90. Sanchez, Claudio. English language learners: How your state is doing. February 2017: https://www.npr.org/sections/ed/2017/02/23/512451228/5-million-english-language-learners-a-vast-pool-of-talent-at-risk.

91. See footnote 65-. University at Albany's Educational Opportunities Program: https://www.albany.edu/eop/.

92. Wall, Alessandra. Life in focus: 9 things that you can do to be a good ally. June 2018: https://lifeinfocussd.com/9-things-good-ally/

93. https://www.weforum.org/agenda/2019/04/business-case-for-diversity-in-the-workplace/

94. See footnote 10.

95. Green, Joshua. **Moral tribes: Emotion, reason, and the gaps between us and them.** New York: Penguin Random House Books. 2013.

96. Akter, Sarmin Eggan, Branden, and Stellar, James. A constant battle: As the amygdala takes on the ventromedial prefrontal cortex. August 2019: http://otherlobe.com/a-constant-battle-as-the-amygdala-takes-on-the-ventromedial-prefrontal-cortex-blog-3/.

97. See footnote 58.

98. Akter, Sarmin, Eggan, Branden, and Stellar, James. A constant battle: Conscious and subconscious brain areas. July 2019: http://otherlobe.com/1079-2/.

99. For information about the Mu Sigma Epsilon, the first multicultural sorority in the United States, visit the following: http://www.msu1981.org/about/.

100. Beard, D. Opponents second-guessed this all muslim girls basketball team. Bad move. February, 2020: https://www.motherjones.com/media/2020/02/recharge-93-all-muslim-girls-basketball-team/

101. See footnote 86.

102. For more information on the Student National Medical Association: https://snma.org/ and the University at Albany Minority Association of Premedical Students: https://albany.campuslabs.com/engage/organization/maps.

103. For more information on the Center for Ethnic, Racial, and Religious Understanding: https://cerru.org/.

104. Nichols, Marc. Sage on the stage or guide on the side. January 2016: https://higheredrevolution.com/sage-on-the-stage-or-guide-on-the-side-d1f7ec8e1573.

105. Steele, Claude. **Whistling Vivaldi: How stereotypes affect us and what we can do.** New York: W.W. Norton & Company, 2010. Note that the title comes from a story in the book where a black man walking past white folks on a Chicago street finds that he can put them at social ease by whistling from the famous classical music piece by the composer Vivaldi.

106. For more information on stereotype threat: https://en.wikipedia.org/wiki/Stereotype_threat#Long-term_and_other_consequences.

107. Claro, S., Paunesku, D., and Dweck, C.S. **Growth mindset tempers the effects of poverty on academic achievement.** *PNAS,* 113(31), 2016, pp 8664-8668 and Boreman, G.D. and Pyne, J. **What if Coleman had known about stereotype threat? How social-psychological theory can help mitigate educational inequality.** *RSF Journal of Social Psychology,* 2(5), 2016, pp 164-185.

108. Community College Survey of Student Engagement. Making connections: Dimensions of student engagement. 2009: https://files.eric.ed.gov/fulltext/ED529077.pdf

109. University at Albany Diversity and Inclusion Plan: https://www.albany.edu/strategicplan/archive/files/Priority-Diversity-Draft.pdf

110. For more information on the imposter syndrome: https://en.wikipedia. org/wiki/Impostor_syndrome and Parkman, A. **The imposter phenomenon in higher education: Incidence and impact.** *Journal of Higher Education Theory and Practice,* 16(1), 2016, pp 51-60.

111. American Council on Higher Education. College-bound students interests in study abroad and other international learning activities: https:// www.acenet.edu/Documents/2008-Student-Poll.pdf.

112. American Council on Education. Senator Paul Simon study abroad program act introduced in senate: https://www.acenet.edu/News-Room/ Pages/Senator-Paul-Simon-Study-Abroad-Program-Act-Introduced-in-Senate.aspx.

113. For more information on Global Brigades: https://www.globalbrigades. org/.

114. For more information on Volunteer Village: https://www.ewb-usa.org/ volunteer-opportunities/.

115. Rose-Berman, I. How college students can bridge American divides: "Study abroad" in Alabama or New York. August, 2019: https://eu.usa-today.com/story/opinion/2019/08/19/heal-democracy-bridge-divides-study-abroad-at-home-column/1997298001/.

116. Weiser, C.S. and Stellar, J.S. Learning while tutoring in writing. December 2020: http://otherlobe.com/learning-while-tutoring-in-writing/.

117. For more on the experiential education blog: www.otherlobe.com.